Published for
Swedish Pioneer Historical Society

by
Southern Illinois University Press
Carbondale and Edwardsville

Feffer & Simons, Inc.
London and Amsterdam

Swedish
Exodus

by Lars Ljungmark

Translated by Kermit B. Westerberg

Photographs of the Olof Krans paintings of the Bishop Hill Colony courtesy of Bishop Hill Heritage Association.

Photograph of the Gethsemane Lutheran Church in Austin courtesy of Carl Widén.

Photograph of "Old Main" courtesy of Augustana College.

All other photographs courtesy of the Emigrant Institute at Växjo.

Library of Congress Cataloging in Publication Data

Ljungmark, Lars.
  Swedish exodus.

  Revised translation of the work published in 1965
under title: Den stora utvandringen.
  Bibliography: p.
  Includes index.
  1. Swedish Americans. 2. United States—
Emigration and immigration. I. Swedish Pioneer
Historical Society. II. Title.
El84.S23L5313   301.32'8'485073   79-10498
ISBN 0-8093-0905-X

Contents

List of Illustrations
and Figures

Illustrations

following page 60

En route to Gothenburg
Posters of Atlantic steamship lines
Portrait of Colonel Hans Mattson
Olof Krans Painting of Bishop Hill
Wilson Line shuttle across North Sea
Swedish lumberjacks felling redwoods
Castle Garden
Sod hut in South Dakota
Homestead in Red River Valley
"Swede Town" in Chicago

following page 104

Emigrant contract
Advertisement for railroad land
Sillgatan (Herring Street) in Gothenburg
Brig loaded with iron bars
Passenger liner "Stockholm"
Emigrant liner in 1920s
"Mr. Coleson's Trip to Sweden"
Olof Krans painting of Bishop Hill
Typical church built by Swedish immigrants
"Old Main," Augustana College

Figures

Foreword

Swedish Exodus is a revision and translation of *Den stora utvandringen,* which appeared in 1965 as a course book for a Swedish radio series led by its author, Lars Ljungmark. It capitalized on the interest aroused in Swedish emigration by the novels of Vilhelm Moberg and led to the formation of hundreds of study circles in continuing-education centers all over Sweden. The radio series was repeated in 1966; the study program continued over a ten-year period, with the author frequently engaged as guest lecturer.

As an example of the impact of the program, in one province alone (Hallands *län*) studies were begun in thirty-three communities with over three hundred lay researchers involved in local emigration history. The interest there carried over to this country, and the end result was a volume, *Halländska emigrant öden 1860–1930* (The Fortunes of Halland Emigrants), that placed the migration from that part of Sweden in a larger perspective.

In 1971, Lars Ljungmark received his doctorate and became a *docent* at Gothenburg University, where he now is associate professor in history. His research, begun in 1958 to explore Captain Hans Mattson's recruitment of Swedes for the state of Minnesota, resulted in the volume, *For Sale—Minnesota,* which appeared in this country under the imprint of the Swedish Pioneer Historical Society.

Swedish Exodus meets the need for a scholarly introduction to Swedish immigration based on the most recent research. This volume adds much to our understanding of an important chapter in the story of the greatest movement of people in human history: the great migration that brought 35 million European immigrants, including 1.25 million Swedes, to these shores in the space of a century and a half.

The Swedish Pioneer Historical Society hopes that *Swedish Exodus* will lead to results similar to those in Sweden and will find use in the classroom and in local historical societies so that a new generation of students and historians will be stimulated to probe the effects of Swedish immigration on their own lives and communities.

Wesley M. Westerberg   Evanston, Illinois
January 1979

Swedish Exodus

1 They Left for America

Today's Swedes unquestionably are the most Americanized people in Europe. Television, movies, and magazines bring them into constant contact with the American life-style and way of thinking. Swedish school children begin to learn English at the age of ten and continue with the language for at least six years. In the early 1600s, however, America loomed for Swedes and other Europeans as the vast, enticing, and unknown continent, the subject of fantastic stories and rumors. The mystery surrounding this continent inspired a sense of adventure that, among other things, led in 1638 to the founding of New Sweden along the shores of the Delaware River. New Sweden remained in Swedish hands for only a short time, falling to the Dutch in 1665.

More than two hundred years after the loss of that first colony, the continent that had become synonymous with the new and expanding world power known as the United States was still the object of many Swedish dreams of success. Yet America remained essentially unknown. Even in educated circles, for example, few Swedes spoke English. One illustration of this dates from 1869 when a party of emigrants sent the following message from Liverpool to relatives in Sweden: "Leave for America today everyone is happy." When translated by the Swedish press the message read: *Lefve Amerika. I dag äro alla lyckliga* (Long live America. Today everyone is happy).[1]

Mass emigration from Sweden has played a very small role in

the Americanization of twentieth-century Sweden. The decisive factors are to be found in American society, including its political, technological, and cultural contributions to world civilization. What the Americanization of modern Sweden has done, however, is spur new interest in the fate of the emigrants who left Sweden. People have begun to ask questions about their distant American relatives in light of what television programs and movies reveal about the American Wild West, the American police and detective world, the American urban ghetto, and the American presidential elections.

In the past most Swedes gave very little thought to their "unknown" relatives on the other side of the Atlantic. It was enough to say that "they left for America." Now that America's past and present have become more familiar, the emigrants themselves seem a lot closer. Emigration again has become a household word for historians as well as for the Swedish public. Some of the success won by Vilhelm Moberg's novels on the emigrant odyssey of Karl Oskar and Kristina probably is due to the intimacy so many people felt with the events and persons Moberg portrayed. They found it easy to associate the main characters with distant and half-forgotten great-uncles and grandparents, who may have made the journey just as Moberg's characters did. Contemporary Swedes also were able to identify with the American setting in these novels because of their exposure to American Wild West films. The America of the nineteenth century as popularized by the mass media, in other words, suddenly became populated with Swedes.

There is, of course, a great deal of difference between Vilhelm Moberg's masterful portrayal of the individual emigrant's fate and the historian's attempt to provide a total perspective on Swedish emigration, including its causes and stages of development. On the other hand, just as Moberg's engaging novels of early Swedish emigrants captured a sweep of emigration history, the historian's factual account also can include attention to the emigrants as persons. In this book the lives of individual emigrants will be illustrated primarily by excerpts from their own letters or by short selections from the autobiographical sketches published in the official report of the Swedish Commission on Emigration in 1908.

The story of this great emigration is the story of how more than one million Swedes, many of whom rarely had ventured outside their native districts, broke with tradition and crossed the Atlantic to settle in a strange and unfamiliar part of the world. Today our rapid means of communication make it difficult for us to share the feelings of these emigrants at the time of their departure. As a rule they were well aware that they would never see their homes again. This was emphasized in their letters home.

> You write that you miss me very much. That is not to be wondered at, because nothing lies closer to the heart than the love between children and parents. But, pray, do not worry too much about me. I got along well in Sweden, and this being a better country, I will do even better here. As my plans are now, I have no desire to be in Sweden. I never expect to speak with you again in this life. . . . Your loving daughter unto death,
>
> Mary Jonson[2]

Swedes have associated several things with the word *emigration*. Aside from the harsh reality of departure, the first "dog years" in a new country and the hope of "striking it rich" stand in the center of attention. These last two elements have also been personified, as in the tragic ballad of Petter Jönsson's rise and fall and the tales of Swedish Americans returning home with gold watch chains on their vests and silver dollars in their pockets (see page 35). From their first landing emigrants faced difficulties. A Swedish clergyman in New York who befriended them wrote in 1865:

> Every day since Brother Esbjörn left I have had to work among the immigrants. A great many are lying ill on Ward's Island; some have died and two women have given birth to children. One of them is reported dead, but I have been unable to visit her, as I live six miles away. The father is out west, and on Ward's Island there is said to be a deserted boy, who runs

about dirty and full of vermin. At Castle Garden there are between twenty and thirty persons without a cent, who tug at my coat and tap my shoulder, crying: " Pastor, get me away from here so that we may escape the poorhouse."[3]

Some success stories had their corollary in disappointment. Jonas August appears to have first struck it rich. His nephew wrote: "We must let you know about the good fortune of Jonas August. He has been mining gold in the Idaho territory, and has in cash four thousand dollars (sixteen thousand *riksdaler*) over and above all expenses. He made all this last summer. It sounds unbelievable, but it is true. I counted the money myself."[4] But six months later another letter reported: "Uncle Sandahl and Jonas Peter are in the goldfields, but they are not mining much gold. Uncle is bothered with backache. They write that they are coming home this fall."[5] The emigrants rarely got anything for free.

Emigration symbolized a break with tradition, a struggle to overcome obstacles, and a dream of success. The emigrants personified a desire for "making a go of it." An illustration of this spirit comes from a letter written in 1907 in which the successful Swedish American cannot refrain from exhibiting his good fortune even in a proposal for marriage:

> Honored Pastor,
>   The undersigned wishes herewith to ask whether the Pastor knows if there is any woman by the name of Anna Katarina Bergstedt. That was her maiden name about twenty-four years ago. . . . If the Pastor would be so kind and inform me where she is I am sending herewith a letter to her in case it should reach her. She lived at Vedlösa at the above-named time and her father was a miller. I am sending the Pastor an America-dollar for the trouble.
>
> > Einar M.

Enclosed was this letter:

> Dear Anna,
>   I wonder how you have it and if you are living. I have it very good here. It is a long time since we saw each other. Are

you married or unmarried? If you are unmarried, you can have a good home with me. I have my own house in town and I make over ten *kronor* a day. My wife died last year in the fall and I want another wife. . . . If you can come to me I will send you a ticket and travel money for the spring when it will be good weather. We live very good here in America. I have been here for fourteen years. . . . You must wonder who I am. My name is Einar, who worked over at Vensta for Adolf Johanson when you were at Andersons', and you were my first girl-friend. . . . If these lines should reach you please write right away and let me know how things are with you. Signed, your old friend Einar. . . .

I will write a few words in English, *j am Loved joy of all my Hart j hav bin driming af bort joy y hoppes dat joy vill bi my vife*

Respechtifulli

Good Bye

j am sand joy one worm kiss[6]

Europeans Transform a New Continent

The history of the United States has been described in terms of a transformation of a "wild and primitive environment" by an old European civilization. The first white settlers were more than just pioneers and explorers: they were the first in a long line of European immigrants who actively transplanted an old culture onto American soil.

The settlement of the North American continent grew with the expansion of the American frontier, which pushed westward from the borders of the former British colonies and halted in 1890 at the shores of the Pacific Ocean. That same year the United States Census Bureau issued the following statement: "Up to and including 1880 the country had a frontier of settlement, but at present the unsettled area has been so broken into by isolated bodies of settlement that there can hardly be said to be a frontier line. In the discussion of its extent and its westward movement it can not, therefore, any longer have a place in the census reports."[7]

The disappearance of the American frontier did not mean that settlements were uniformly distributed on the map. Large areas were still uncultivated, and there was plenty of open space for industrious and land-hungry pioneers. To complete the settlement of the entire nation would have been impossible for the American population of 5.3 million in 1800. Help was needed, and it would come from the other side of the Atlantic. Mass emigration from Europe stimulated the process of nation building and led to record population growth. Of the 63 million residents of the United States in 1890, 21 million were first- or second-generation European immigrants.

The Great Immigration Waves

It was in the late 1840s that European immigrants began on a large scale to participate in western colonization. New waves of immigrants followed in their footsteps, and evidences of their settlements can still be seen along successive frontiers. In this respect, it was more often the timing of immigrant arrivals in the United States, and not the possible similarities to the geography of native countries, that decided where they would settle.

Figure 1 shows that there were definite peaks in the course of European immigration to America. The first major wave came between 1847 and 1856, at a time when the frontier had reached the Mississippi Valley and the states on either side of the Central Mississippi region were pioneer territory. During this one decade 3 million people immigrated to the United States—twice as many as during the previous seventy-year period. Most of these immigrants came from Great Britain, Ireland and Germany, the Irish increasing in numbers as a result of the potato famine in Ireland in 1845–46.

The second major wave swept over the United States from 1865 to 1873 and included for the first time large numbers of Scandinavians. By this time the frontier had extended to the Upper Mississippi Valley, and the states of Illinois, Wisconsin, Iowa, and Minnesota virtually became Scandinavian settlements.

Following a decline in immigration, caused by economic recession in the United States, the third major wave burst on the scene from 1880 to 1893. During this period 7.3 million people immigrated, mainly as a result of the agricultural crisis in

Figure 1. Immigration to the United States, 1841–1960. Decade Averages.

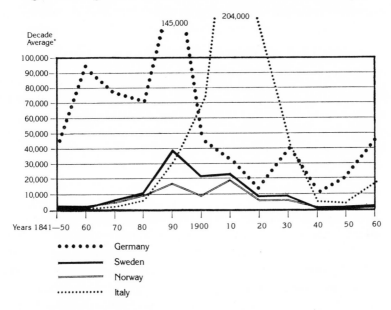

*Decade averages represent total emigration per decade divided by ten, based on United States immigration statistics.

Europe. This was the last of the "old immigration waves," dominated by such groups as the Irish, English, Scots, Germans, and Scandinavians. By this time the frontier had pushed farther west to the Plains States of Colorado, Nebraska, Kansas, and the Dakotas, which became the haven for countless land-hungry immigrants.

During this settlement wave, representatives of the "new immigration" from southern and eastern Europe began to arrive in large numbers and take their places alongside the northern Europeans. These new immigrants completely dominated the last and largest wave of transatlantic movement between 1900 and 1914. No less than 13.4 million people immigrated during these years, primarily from Russia—including Poles and Jews— the Austro-Hungarian Empire, and Italy. In contrast to the earlier immigrants, these groups settled largely in the eastern

United States, as their arrival coincided more or less with the forces of industrialization and urbanization in American society.

The Halt of Mass Immigration

While the outbreak of World War I checked the momentum of European emigration, it also set the stage for the final phase of mass immigration to the United States. The decisive factors were not the changes in European society but rather the changes in American attitudes to mass immigration. The upsurge of nationalism that preceded and followed America's entrance into the war played a significant role in this context. Americans discovered that they were in no way a homogeneous nation but rather a mosaic of different European nationalities, which included large numbers of Germans. This prompted the decision to close the doors on further immigration and in the process build an "American" nation. A contributing factor was the opposition from labor groups to the growing ranks of job-hungry immigrants who, in their eyes, showed no solidarity with American workers during strikes and lockouts. The result was a series of restrictive immigration laws, capped by the Immigration Act of 1924 and its amendments of 1929, which fixed a limit of 150,000 immigrants per year, with the exception of those from North and South America. Below this maximum level a quota system determined the number of immigrants admissible from each country. Despite the favoritism shown to immigrants from northern Europe, the quota restrictions obstructed any further mass immigration from these countries. The stock market crash of 1929 and the depression of the 1930s soon made the United States less attractive to immigrants. Since that time immigration from northern Europe has averaged only one-fifth of its assigned quotas, and therefore one can say that mass European immigration came to a halt by 1930.

The Causes of Immigration

What was responsible for this tremendous migration of over 31 million Europeans to American shores? The explanations are to be found on both sides of the Atlantic, and a number of factors deserve attention.

The Europeans who left for America before the start of mass emigration in the 1840s had one thing in common: all of them were turning their backs on something. In other words, primarily negative factors in home countries initially prompted people to make the long and hazardous journey across the Atlantic. Usually it was a reaction to a climate of political and religious intolerance in early nineteenth-century Europe.

The growing pace of industrialization also caused economic unrest, such as sharp fluctuations in business cycles that led to periods of unemployment and price crashes. This unrest was often connected with a population boom resulting from a relaxation of such demographic threats as warfare, pestilence, and famine; or, as the Swedish poet and bishop, Esaias Tegner, once described it, an era of "peace, vaccination, and potatoes." In most countries these conditions led to overpopulation, which plagued the economy and intensified the effects of occasional crop failures, despite the introduction of potato cultivation. The widespread potato famine in Ireland, which caused the first mass emigration to the United States, offers a prime example.

These motivating factors in European society were enhanced, at the other end of the scale, by European interest in the Enlightenment ideals of the early American republic. The United States represented a positive contrast to European conditions and loomed as a model country for all who suffered at the hands of reactionary governments, ruthless employers, and meagre living conditions. The combination, then, of push factors in Europe and pull factors in America gave rise to mass emigration in which growing scores of Europeans turned toward something—the new United States.

The start of mass emigration during the 1840s emphasized the significance of purely economic factors for would-be emigrants. Concrete examples include the California gold rush of 1848 and the promise of free land under the Homestead Act of 1862. Yet these isolated factors fail to explain the entire movement between 1847 and 1930. The only suitable explanation is to be found in the general conviction that America was the promised land for material success. Once this conviction had been amplified by supporters of increased immigration—that is, the American immigration industry—and transatlantic travel became cheaper and simpler, mass emigration was a reality.

Emigration also had the capacity to reproduce itself, along the lines of a chain reaction. Early emigrants created situations that led to further emigration. They cultivated more and more land in America and added new sections of track to the nation's railroads. This caused a surplus of cheap American wheat in Europe and a deterioration in the economic conditions for European farmers, thereby adding fuel to the emigration process.

All of these factors varied in strength at different times and were responsible for the peaks and valleys in the emigration curve. Economic factors had the greatest instability, and the fluctuations between prosperity and recession on both sides of the Atlantic determined most of the changes in the intensity of emigration.

Extent of Swedish Immigration

Of eight leading immigration nationalities (Germany, Ireland, Great Britain, Sweden, Norway, Italy, Austria, and Russia), Sweden, with its 1.25 million emigrants, ranks seventh on the list but leads all of the Scandinavian countries in absolute figures. If one looks at relative figures–comparing emigration to population statistics–Norway far surpasses Sweden. After Ireland, Norway is the one country that experienced the greatest emigration in relation to its population. During the period 1880–1900, when Swedish emigration reached its peak, the rate of emigrants leaving Sweden (number of emigrants in relation to population) was three times the median for all of Europe. Only Ireland and Norway had larger relative figures at this time.

The extent of Swedish emigration is shown by Figure 2. The growth curve of Swedish emigration is not strikingly different from that of other Scandinavian countries except that mass Swedish emigration began somewhat later. According to official Swedish statistics a total of 1,122,292 Swedes emigrated to

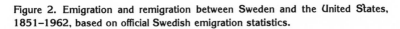

Figure 2. Emigration and remigration between Sweden and the United States, 1851–1962, based on official Swedish emigration statistics.

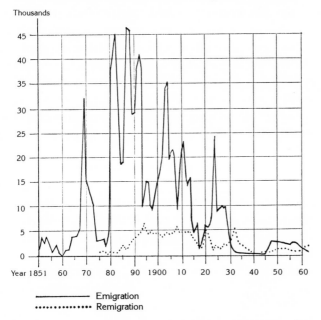

—————— Emigration
•••••••••••• Remigration

America from 1851 to 1930. These statistics are too low because of a high number of unregistered emigrants. With the aid of passenger lists from ports of embarkation, current researchers are trying to determine the exact number of Swedish emigrants. Four specific years have been chosen for intensive study, but the only results available at this time are for the year 1874. These show that the new statistics exceed the official ones by no less than 40 percent. This does not mean, however, that research can correct the situation by adding these figures to the official totals. The passenger list statistics on annual emigration also are misleading in that they record visiting Swedish Americans as emigrants. Drawing on what is known at this point, research has estimated very approximately that unregistered emigration for the entire 1851–1930 period totaled one hundred thousand persons. This means that up to 1.25 million Swedes emigrated during that period.

The greatest number of Swedish-born residents in the United

States was recorded in 1910—approximately six hundred sixty-five thousand adults and approximately seven hundred thousand children. The combined total of approximately 1.37 million is given sharper focus when compared to the home Swedish population in about 1910, which was then around 5.5 million. In other words, about one-fifth of the world's Swedish population was living in America.

The first inkling of an emigration wave came in the early 1850s. An average of about three thousand persons per year emigrated between 1852 and 1854. Emigration declined during the latter part of that decade but rose again steadily during the early 1860s, reaching a peak in 1869. Mass emigration began in 1868, and in the next five years one hundred three thousand Swedes left for America. Crop failures in Sweden at a time when free land was available in America and reports of great prosperity in the republic across the sea inspired the exodus.

These conditions were reversed later which led to a decline in emigration, but a new surge developed in 1879. Over the next fourteen years, up to 1894, an average of approximately thirty-four thousand Swedes emigrated annually. Figure 2 shows, however, that this emigration did not remain at a constant level but fluctuated to a relatively high degree.

Fluctuating economic developments in Sweden and America were primarily responsible for this major emigration wave. While conditions were deteriorating in Sweden, especially for farmers, the United States was enjoying a tide of economic prosperity. At the same time the propaganda campaign launched in the late 1860s to encourage emigration began to bear fruit. An average of nearly forty-six thousand Swedes emigrated annually.

According to official statistics 493,000 Swedes emigrated from 1879 to 1893. When the mass emigration era came to a close in 1930, statistics showed that approximately 40 percent of all Swedish emigrants left during the peak years of the 1880s. Emigration declined at the very end of the nineteenth century, just as it did during the 1870s and for roughly the same reason—improved conditions in Sweden.

Official statistics show that 289,000 Swedes emigrated to

America from 1900 to 1913: this amounted to half of the movement's strength during the peak period between 1879 and 1893. Two minor peaks are recorded, however, during the years leading up to World War I: one came in 1902–03 and another, smaller one, in 1910. Both were caused by crises affecting Swedish industry and the Swedish labor market. In 1909 Sweden suffered its only major labor conflict, the so-called Great Strike.

Remigration to Sweden increased during the last decades of the 1800s and past the turn of the century. The twenty-year period up to World War I saw an annual remigration of approximately four- to five-thousand persons. In other words, a little over 20 percent of the emigrants returned to Sweden. While World War I placed an effective barrier on emigration, remigration continued to take place. As a result, the net loss to Sweden for the decade 1911 to 1920 was only about forty-four thousand persons, which was the lowest it had been since the 1850s.

After World War I restrictive legislation in America began to affect emigration. A final peak came in 1923, when record unemployment in Sweden caused close to twenty-five thousand persons to leave the country. Emigration remained at a level of about nine thousand per year up to the stock market crash of 1929, when remigration surpassed emigration for the first time since the war. This was to be the pattern for the future. At no time during the 1930s did emigration reach the one-thousand level, which represented one-third of the approximately three-thousand emigrant quota assigned to Sweden by the law of 1925 that became effective in 1929.

During the 1940s a total of 10,924 Swedes emigrated to the United States, the majority arriving after the end of World War II. Swedish emigration during the 1950s accounted for approximately twenty-three thousand five hundred persons, which on the average represented slightly more than three-fourths of the assigned annual quota. The annual average for the 1960s and 1970s has been in the vicinity of seventeen hundred persons. As a rule, immigration to Sweden from the United States has been higher.

2 Group Emigration from Sweden and Stage Migration in the United States

Prior to the first mass emigration wave in 1868, Swedish emigration was largely characterized by movements of distinct groups of people. Some of them came from the same village or province, while others were led by a prominent personality. All of them have several features in common: they were led by a central figure, almost all of the members in each group came from the same general area of Sweden, and all of them founded colonies in the Middle West.

The Student from Uppsala

Gustaf Unonius, an Uppsala University student, was typical of the individuals often found among the early Swedish emigrants to the United States. He came from a good social background and saw America in romantic terms as the vision of the future. This was the result of his extensive university education in such areas as military science, law, and medicine. His view of America was strongly reminiscent of the French philosopher Jean Jacques Rousseau's naturalistic thinking, which several decades earlier had prompted the Swedish author Carl Jonas Love Almquist to settle down in the dense forests of Värmland. Unonius's own decision to emigrate was directly influenced by his unsuccessful attempts as an author. At the same time, however, he was highly motivated by what he knew of the recent Norwegian and German immigration to the American Middle West.

14

Unonius's decision to leave Sweden with his young wife caused a stir of excitement in the university town of Uppsala. In fact, two other students, their maid, and dog Fille joined the Unonius household in May, 1841, when they left Gävle on a brig bound for New York with a cargo of iron. Although the group had not decided on a specific location, the ultimate goal seemed to be the Midwest.

After securing advice and information in New York, they decided to settle in Illinois. During the journey west by canal boat, however, they changed their minds and finally settled near Pine Lake, about five miles west of Milwaukee, Wisconsin. From our twentieth-century vantage point it is easy to find fault with their preference for the wilds of Wisconsin as opposed to the relatively well-settled state of Illinois. The surroundings were far from ideal.

During the next four years the New Uppsala or Pine Lake colony became the destination of emigrants from the same social class as Unonius. They were people wo found themselves at odds with Swedish society, either as a result of frivolous living and bad company, or because of dashed hopes of good careers, or even for reasons of adventure alone. For all of them the vision of a free America appeared as a solution to their problems.

The Pine Lake colony did not last long. This group of former university students, merchants, and military officers lacked the physical stamina needed for frontier life. The land was hard to cultivate and gave little in return. In time the colony's residents went their separate ways. Only six Swedish families were still living in the area when Fredrika Bremer, the famous Swedish author, visited the colony in September, 1850. She described what she saw:

> We sailed along the tree-lined shores which reflected their gladsome autumn colors in the looking-glass lake. Here, on a high promontory, ablaze with foliage, New Uppsala would stand! These were the words of Unonius and his friends when they first set foot in this wild, untamed place and were taken by its beauty. Alas—the wilderness would not bear Uppsala's sons! I saw the abandoned homes where Unonius and Schneidau had struggled against all odds, in vain.[1]

Unonius became a priest in the American Episcopal Church, but returned to Sweden in 1858, where he eventually took a post as customs supervisor in Grisslehamn. Before that he had tried unsuccessfully for the priesthood in the Swedish state church, but in 1862 he published his *Minnen från en sjuttonårig vistelse i nordvestra Amerika* (published in English as *A Pioneer in Northwest America 1841–1858*), one of Sweden's classic works of emigrant literature. Gustaf Unonius's role in the history of Swedish emigration had greater significance than his short-lived Wisconsin settlement might lead one to believe. During his years at Pine Lake he wrote numerous letters to Swedish newspapers, primarily the liberal *Aftonbladet,* as a means of improving his stringent economic situation. Despite Unonius's bitter experiences, his letters painted an idealized picture of the Pine Lake colony and American life in general, and they proved to have considerable significance as stimulants to new emigrants.

The Master Builder from Kisa

Unonius was not the only correspondent in the Pine Lake colony. Lieutenant Polycarpus von Schneidau was another, and his letters were the first to bear fruit in Sweden. Originally addressed to his father in the Kisa area of Östergötland, von Schneidau's letters were later copied and circulated throughout the countryside. Among this larger and enthusiastic readership was the fifty-five-year-old farmer, miller, and master builder, Peter Cassel, who in 1845 led a group of seventeen Kisa residents across the Atlantic to Wisconsin.

The difference between Unonius and Cassel was the difference between the romantic intellectual and the practical-minded leader. True, both of them reached a decision to emigrate on the basis of what they had read about America, but von Schneidau's letters contained far more practical information than the literature responsible for Unonius's view of America. Cassel also went to great lengths in preparing for his journey. He studied English, made a conscious effort to learn more about the new country, and selected his companions with great care.

It has often been said that Cassel left Sweden primarily for political reasons. He was definitely a member of the liberal opposition in Swedish politics, and in Kisa he had signed a petition in support of parliamentary reform. But in his case there were other reasons as well. Aside from his decidedly liberal sympathies, he had the reputation of being a warm temperance supporter and a free-church leader, and he was said to have a clear and often outspoken opinion on the economic problems facing Swedish farmers, especially high taxes. It is not true, however, that Cassel's temperance convictions and free-church involvement isolated him from the local population. Several prominent persons in Kisa, including the local priest, were his staunch supporters. What one does find in Cassel is a sincere conviction that America was a better country on all accounts. If Cassel did harbor any personal grudges toward Sweden they were probably not the reason why he organized a party of American emigrants or why he continued to attract others from the Kisa area. It is more likely that in his leadership capacity, Cassel sought to provide better living conditions for his immediate followers.

After their arrival in New York, Cassel and his party learned that all of the prime farm land in Wisconsin had already been taken. Together with one additional family, they decided to try their fortunes in Iowa. From New York they traveled by rail to Philadelphia; then by canal boat to Pittsburgh, where they boarded a river steamer for the journey down the Ohio River and up the Mississippi to Burlington, Iowa; and finally on foot seven miles northwest to the Skunk River, where they founded the New Sweden colony.

The party's social background made it well suited for pioneer life, and the colony had a far brighter future than Unonius's Pine Lake settlement. In 1858, a year after Cassel's death, New Sweden boasted a population of five hundred Swedes, including a hundred families. This was primarily the result of direct emigration from Sweden which, in turn, stemmed from Cassel's foremost contribution to emigration history, his own "America letters." Most of these letters were published in the Swedish press and consequently received a wide readership, as the Swedish public attached great importance to the fact that the New Sweden colony was composed of more "ordinary" people than those who founded the Pine Lake settlement. Even more important for this wide publicity was the position of the liberal Swedish press, which regarded emigration as a suitable means of protesting the deplorable conditions in Swedish society.

Like Unonius's letters, Cassel's contained highly positive impressions of the colony and America as a whole. Their effect on potential emigration extended beyond the confines of Kisa and the province of Östergötland. People found it hard to resist such descriptions as these:

> The ease of making a living here and the increasing prosperity of the farmers, year by year and day by day, exceeds anything we anticipated. If only half of the work expended on the soil in the fatherland were utilized here, the yield would reach the wildest imaginations. . . . All crops thrive and grow to an astonishing degree. Cornfields are more like woods than grain fields. . . .
>
> Freedom and equality are the fundamental principles of the Constitution of the United States. There is no such thing as class distinction here, no courts, barons, lords, or lordly estates. The one is as good as another, and everyone lives in the unrestricted enjoyment of personal liberty.[2]

The Prophet from Biskopskulla (Bishop Hill)

Erik Jansson, known as "the prophet" from Biskopskulla parish, north of Enköping in Uppland province, had only one reason for leading his followers across the Atlantic: freedom from religious persecution. Although born in Uppland, Jansson grew up in Västmanland province, and he sold his farm in Österunda parish in 1844 and moved to Hälsingland province, where he had his largest following. As a flour salesman and lay preacher, he had travelled extensively in Hälsingland and neighboring provinces beginning in 1842. By moving to Hälsingland he hoped to have closer contact with large numbers of the *läsare* (lay readers), who met in homes to read and discuss the Bible and devotional writings and to pray together—most often age. Their reasons were partly a zest for adventure and partly the knowledge that wealth and social standing had too much influence if a career would be successful in Sweden. For several years after his arrival Mattson tried his hand at different jobs and went through the process of finding himself. In 1853 he made his home in Moline, Illinois, where he was joined by the rest of the family. A fluent knowledge of English and a natural gift for leadership encouraged him in August 1853 to head a small group of Swedes anxious to find land farther west in Minnesota.

Mattson and his party first traveled by river steamer to St. Paul, where they made inquiries about settlement possibilities. From there Mattson and two of his companions made their way down the Mississippi again to the small trading post at Red Wing, populated at the time by a handful of white settlers and a tribe of Sioux Indians. They found what they were looking for along a tributary of the Mississippi two miles west of Red Wing and staked their claim to an area. After consultations with the rest of the party, it was decided that Mattson, Gustav Kempe from Västergötland, and Carl Roos from Värmland would spend the winter on the new claim. The winter was cold but short, and by early April the group had already begun spring planting.

Throughout the spring and summer the number of log cabins increased. After another year, in September 1855, came Erik Norelius, who had served as a Lutheran minister among Swedes in northwestern Indiana. By this time the colony had a population of some hundred Swedes; this was enough to form a congregation, which received the name "Vasa." The name was attractive enough, and the colony soon adopted it as its own; up to that time it had simply been called "Mattson's Settlement." Mattson began to promote the colony by writing letters to the Swedish-American newspaper, *Hemlandet,* which had subscribers on both sides of the Atlantic. This publicity, coupled with private correspondence from the Vasa colonists, led to a steady stream of immigrants over the next several years. The new arrivals were a mixed group: some immigrated directly from Sweden, while others filtered in from the East Coast as Swedish-American pioneers. Mattson himself, as he writes in his *Reminiscences,* found the "world becoming too narrow on the

without benefit of clergy and frequently in conflict with them. There he soon formed a sect of his own called the Erik Janssonists, who believed that it was possible for the believer immediately to live a sinless life. In opposition to the Lutheran position on such matters, the Janssonists went so far as to hold book burnings of devotional literature, such as the writings of Luther and Arndt, setting themselves at odds with the administration of law and order. The Janssonists became the target of repeated court hearings and official persecutions, and Jansson himself was arrested on numerous occasions and spent most of his time between 1844 and early 1846 in prison. During this time the sect began to give serious consideration to the idea of emigration, and it received some encouragement from the letters of earlier emigrants.

Among Jansson's most devoted followers were two brothers from Söderala, Olof and Jonas Olsson. Once the Janssonists had reached a decision to emigrate, Olof Olsson left for America in the fall of 1845 to make preparations for their arrival and, above all, to choose a suitable site for a settlement. In New York, Olsson consulted with the Methodist preacher Olof Gustaf Hedström, whose unrigged "Bethel Ship" lay anchored in lower Manhattan harbor. From the ship, Hedström spread Methodist teachings among newly-arrived emigrants and also provided them with practical information about travel routes and likely settlement locations. After his talk with Hedström, Olsson decided to make his way to Illinois, where Hedström's brother, Jonas, a blacksmith and wagon maker, also functioned as a lay preacher. Once in Illinois, Olsson, with Jonas Hedström's help, chose a site in Henry County, approximately 140 miles southwest of Chicago.

Meanwhile Erik Jansson had been arrested in Hälsingland for the sixth time and sent by special transport to the city prison in Gävle. En route he managed to escape to Norway, and later, by way of Copenhagen, Hamburg, and Liverpool, he sailed to New York with his family. He arrived in Illinois in the summer of 1846, when he, Olof Olsson, and a small group of earlier arrivals purchased the land in Henry County.

During the last series of persecutions, capped by Jansson's

trial and prison sentence, the Janssonists began to regard themselves as the new children of Israel. Emigration to America became the counterpart to the Jewish exodus into the land of Canaan. Erik Jansson's safe arrival in Illinois was all that was needed to put these plans into motion. Janssonists in Hälsingland and neighboring provinces sold their farms and placed their money in a collective fund, which enabled even the poorest of the sect to make the journey. Before the end of the year approximately four hundred persons had arrived in the New Jerusalem in Henry County, Illinois, which took the name of Bishop Hill after the "prophet's" own birthplace in Uppland. In the spring of 1847, another four hundred persons arrived. In all, between twelve hundred and fifteen hundred Janssonists left Sweden, although the population of Bishop Hill never reached more than eight hundred.

The newly established colony sent positive and encouraging words to followers in Sweden. In February, 1847, for example, one letter read: "I can now inform you that the word has been made perfect in our midst and that all of our adversaries' prophecies have come to naught. For the land which we have taken is vast and wide. It is a land of plenty for earthly souls, brimming over with milk and honey, as prophesied in Jeremiah 3:19."[3] Over the next several years, the Janssonists made their way to America from such harbors as Gävle, Söderhamn, Stockholm, Gothenburg, and Christiana (Oslo). Not all of them arrived safely. One ship sank shortly after departure, another shipwrecked off the coast of Labrador, and one shipload was decimated by cholera on the Great Lakes.

The first winter in Illinois was extremely difficult, with people living together in dug-outs built into the sides of a ravine; but at its end the settlers set about their new tasks with incredible energy and self-assurance. They broke the land, built houses, and started numerous profitable industries, including textiles, blacksmithing, wagonmaking, furniture, lumber, and milling. In 1858 the colony owned about fourteen thousand acres. Bishop Hill was a collective society where all inhabitants owned a share of the property. This was due partially to the sect's ideal of life and partially to necessity. Their houses followed the same collective principles and were built in masterly fashion from hand-molded brick. A good example is provided by the so-called Brick House completed in 1851, with kitchens and dining rooms on the ground floor and, on the three upper levels, seventy large rooms for single-family dwellings. Another structure which, in physical appearance, has often stood as a symbol of Bishop Hill, is the Steeple Building from 1854. These buildings have generally withstood the test of time and have in recent years undergone extensive restoration. Today the contrast between these imposing structures and those of the small surrounding community still reminds visitors of their collective origins.

These positive details, however, do not tell half of the story. By the end of the 1850s the sect was already in a state of dissolution. Disease, early withdrawals due to Erik Jansson's dictatorial leadership, and factionalism after his death had taken their toll. In May 1850 Jansson was murdered over a dispute about a marriage arrangement between his cousin and an outsider. After that the colony was managed in a more democratic fashion, primarily as a collective. Communal ownership of all property was still in force, but the new leadership soon began to speculate in capitalistic enterprises such as railroads, housing projects, coal mines, real estate ventures, wild cat banking. As a result, the general economic crisis of 1857 dealt a severe blow to the colony and forced its leadership to draw substantial loans on the original mortgages. The rest of the colony lost faith in its leadership, and in 1860 the final struggle for control began. The collective ownership principle was abandoned, and the colony property was divided among the remaining settlers. A court case was entered against the trustees, but after a decade in the court it was never resolved.

The Minnesota Pioneer from Önnestad

The last group of immigrants typify the staggered westward movement of Swedish Americans, which ran parallel to emigration directly from Sweden to the Middle West. In May 1851 the nineteen-year-old Hans Mattson, from Önnestad outside Kristianstad in Skåne, sailed to America with a friend of the same

farm," and left Vasa in 1856.[4] At that time the Vasa colony had a population of some two hundred Swedes.

Over the years since 1856, Vasa has preserved its genuine Swedish flavor. This does not mean that all of the original settlers and their descendants remained in the area. Rather, Vasa is a typical example of frontier settlements that functioned as "mother colonies" or "way stations" for travelers on the road west. Mattson was not the only original Vasa settler to move on. In fact, he attracted many others from the area during the course of his career as a pioneer leader. What has preserved the Swedish flavor of Vasa is, instead, the fact that other Swedes moved in to take the places of the first settlers. Migrants moving westward generally did so in steps, from Sweden to some settled community, and then on to some new location.

Swedish Americans Go West

At different times nearly all the states from the East to the West Coast saw the emergence of stable Swedish settlements or "emigrant transit stations" similar to the Vasa colony. One example is provided by the New Sweden, Maine, colony established in 1870 by the former American vice consul in Gothenburg, later American minister in Stockholm, W. W. Thomas. The first group of settlers came directly from Sweden as a result of Thomas's contacts. Later moves by second-generation Swedes provided many New England cities and towns with their own Swedish populations.

Another example of a stable Swedish settlement from the eastern United States is Chandler Valley, Pennsylvania, where a Swedish colony called Swedesburg, later Hessel Valley, was founded in the 1840s. Over the course of the next few decades Swedes from this colony filtered into Pennsylvania and New York State. In Illinois, Bishop Hill also functioned as the mother colony of Swedes in the western part of the state. The prime example, however, is Chicago, which funneled Swedes to all parts of the Middle West.

In time "daughter colonies" often acquired their own off-spring farther west. During the 1850s, for example, Swedes from Galesburg, Illinois, settled in counties north of Des Moines, Iowa. This became the site of a post office called Boxholm, named after the town of Boxholm in southern Östergötland. The Boxholm Swedes later resettled in the northwestern part of Iowa.

In many cases daughter colonies resulted from the simple resettlement of family and friends from the original colony farther east; however, there were also organized settlement projects. In the 1880s Swedes from Ishpeming in Marquette County, Michigan, settled in Kingsburg, California, some 150 miles north of Los Angeles. This became the state's largest concentration of rural Swedes. In 1868 a number of newly arrived Chicago Swedes founded the First Swedish Agricultural Company of McPherson County, Kansas. This enterprise acquired some thirteen thousand acres of Union Pacific Railroad land and before the end of the year began to settle in the Smoky Hill River area of Kansas. One of the leaders was Sven A. Lindell from Barkeryd in Småland, and it is partially to his credit that the colony received the name of Lindsborg. In 1869 the Kansas settlement received about one hundred Värmland emigrants, led by a priest in the Swedish state church, Olof Olsson from Sunnemo. Olsson had decided to emigrate after controversies with his superiors, and once in Lindsborg he founded the Bethany Swedish Evangelical Lutheran Church. Several years later, in 1876, Olsson left Lindsborg to accept the post of professor of theology at Augustana College and Seminary in Rock Island, Illinois. His successor was Carl Aaron Swensson, who founded Bethany College in the 1880s and started the Bethany Oratorio Society, which became famous for its annual performances of Handel's Messiah at Easter time.

The farther west one travels in the United States the more examples one finds of pioneer settlements that owe their origins to successive moves by Swedish immigrants. In other words, these were people who had their first taste of America in the East or Middle West. Once they had settled in their new homes out West, they often encouraged direct immigration from their old home districts in Sweden. The Minnesota Swedes, for example, resettled in the rich farming areas along the Washington border in northwestern Idaho and later attracted people from the Östmark region in Värmland.

Direct group immigration from Sweden was the pattern until the American Civil War, while stage migration in groups occurred throughout the mass emigration era. Up until 1900 this was almost exclusively a westward movement, but after that, direct migration on a mass scale often took place to the eastern United States, to such expanding industrial centers as Worcester and Boston, Massachusetts, or New York City.

The Significance of Group Emigration

The difficulties encountered by the very first emigrants supply the best explanation for the rise of group emigration. Those who traveled alone were clearly handicapped from the moment of their departure to the hour of their arrival in the new country. The mass emigration era owed much of its development to group travel, which in America became synonymous with settlement in distinct colonies. The Middle West was fairly dotted with Swedish settlements that retained their ties with the old country either through letters or personal contact. These settlements served as magnets for future immigration.

Most of the early emigrants left with the knowledge that they were turning their backs on something. For some it was the Swedish class system and a reactionary government; for others, personal misfortunes and economic ruin; for others still, religious persecution. Many emigrants, however, also had something to look forward to, or at least thought they did. Expectations of financial success—the possibility of a "lucky strike" or lucrative investment—were an integral part of nearly every decision to emigrate, and in some cases such expectations were the only considerations that really mattered. Some of this thinking was probably uppermost in the minds of Peter Cassel and his followers from Kisa in Östergötland. That so many of the early emigrants came from a relatively affluent social class and had access to investment capital indicates the Cassel party was not unique in this respect. The early emigration from the Karlskoga mining districts in Örebro *län* illustrates this very well.

In 1849 four persons left the Karlskoga area to look for gold in America. One of them was a miner's son by the name of Erik Pettersson. Unlike his traveling companions, Pettersson did not make a rush for the gold fields but drifted about the South and Middle West. After working during the winter of 1850–51 as a lumberjack in the forests along the St. Croix River, he staked his claim to land on the Wisconsin side, where the Mississippi flows into Lake Pepin. From Wisconsin, Pettersson wrote to his brother Jakob, encouraging him and others to join him. In 1853 Jakob did just that by organizing a small emigrant party for the voyage to Wisconsin. Instead of awaiting their arrival, Erik left for Sweden himself and convinced another group of emigrants to make the westward journey in 1854. The result of their initiatives was the Stockholm settlement in Wisconsin, and in the process of settling this area, the Karlskoga emigrants added a new chapter to the history of emigration from Örebro *län*. Of the approximately 350 persons who left for America in 1853–54, no less than 256 came from the Karlskoga area. Investment capital was no problem, as all of them had sold their Karlskoga farms before departure.

Some Swedish districts developed an "emigration tradition" due to the impact of early emigrant departures or the influence of key individuals. In such cases emigration became a frequent alternative to migration within Sweden, specifically the movement from the countryside to the cities that began in the second half of the 1800s. Many hesitated to make a complete break with their rural surroundings and accept the conditions of life in urban areas that lay closer to home. For them the transatlantic journey to Swedish settlements in the Middle West was not a step into a strange and frightening world, but rather a span between two soils, the Swedish and the American. Peter Cassel and Erik Jansson exemplify this phenomenon: both generated an emigration tradition that set a pattern for years to come in their home districts. In many cases this tradition offers the only explanation for the variations of emigration intensity in different parts of Sweden. The initiatives taken by Erik Pettersson and his brother Jakob in 1853–54, for example, had a lasting affect on emigration from Örebro *län* and their native Karlskoga. In 1887 no less than 53 percent of those who left the district made their way to the United States. Mass Swedish emigration would never have materialized without the trailblazing example of the early emigrants and their faithful contacts with people back home.

3   Mass Emigration from Sweden

The Flight from the Countryside

I came to the realization that there was not the remotest chance
of ever owning an inch of Swedish soil if I stayed where I was
and that my only prospects were new trials and tribulations and
the same bitter struggle for survival. Under the circumstances,
then, I chose the lesser of two evils.

All Illinois resident who emigrated
from Halland in 1903.[1]

Since my last letter a little rain has fallen and refreshed the
arid soil. But before that we had several nights of frost which
must have damaged crops in many places. Farmers here are
constantly asking: "How will we manage until next winter, if
our crops fail us this year, too?"

Erik Norelius's comments during
a visit to Sweden in 1868.

Around 1880 the effects of the 1873 panic in America began to
taper off, and a golden era was ushered in. Along with it came
the "America fever," which hit me every single year.

An Illinois resident who
emigrated from Kalmar *län*.[2]

Up to around 1890 the majority of Swedish emigrants came
from rural areas and therefore had close ties to farming. After
that the number of urban emigrants, especially those from in-
28

dustrial centers, increased sharply. Statistics show that the ratio between these two emigrant groups during the greater part of the nineteenth century was 3.5:1 in favor of rural emigrants. During the last five years of mass emigration before World War I the ratio stood at an even 1:1. Since World War I the industrial emigrant category has always been the larger of the two.

The early dominance of rural emigrants reflects the position of agriculture in the Swedish economy during the 1800s. In 1850 agriculture and related occupations employed nearly 78 percent of the Swedish population. Fifty years later the figure was 54 percent. In 1850 no less than 90 percent of the Swedish population lived in the countryside; in 1900, 75 percent. Swedish occupation statistics from the 1800s make it somewhat difficult to determine the exact intensity of emigration among these two population sectors. Up until 1900, however, it seems that rural residents did not have any higher emigration intensity than did residents of urban industrial areas. During the first two decades of this century the intensity was somewhat higher for the urban category, although conditions were not the same throughout Sweden.

Economic factors had a great deal of bearing on the development of mass Swedish emigration, particularly in rural areas faced with overpopulation and insufficient acreage. Sweden's situation was hardly unique, for the same conditions were felt all over Europe at this time. Scientific discoveries, improved medical care, better food, and long periods of peace had lowered the death rate but kept the birth rate at the same high level as before. Sweden had one of the lowest death rates in all of Europe, and despite emigration, its population swelled from 2.3 million in 1800 to around 5.5 million in 1910.

This population boom took dramatic proportions among the lower classes in the Swedish countryside, where growing numbers of landless farm hands, farm workers, small cottagers, and free lodgers filled the ranks of an agricultural proletariat. Despite an ambitious program of land reclamation during the first half of the 1800s, the demand for new acreage exceeded the supply. At the same time the size of landowners' property had been reduced through subdivisions connected with sales transac-

tions and inheritances. During the 1850s the agricultural proletariat made up 40 percent of the entire population. A century
earlier it had been 20 percent. The situation of agricultural
workers was made even worse by new decrees affecting farm
acreage. The traditional village framework was broken up to
allow each farmer access to a uniform allotment of land. In this
process the collective land holdings in each village were divided
among private landowners, and this placed greater restrictions
on the ability of cottagers and free lodgers to provide for themselves. In the past they had been allowed access to pastureland
and timber, even though they had no legal right to these
privileges.

The oversupply of manpower depreciated the wages of landless farm workers, and small-scale farmers struggled with insufficient acreage. For both groups the only solution was to leave
the countryside, either by migrating to industrial cities and
urban areas, or by emigrating to open farmland in America.
Some persons chose both alternatives in succession, moving first
to Swedish cities and later, when their hopes went unfulfilled,
choosing emigration as a final solution. The majority, however,
settled for one alternative and followed it through. An important factor in this context was the rise of a distinct emigration
tradition: internal migration held little attraction in districts
where "America fever" had made strong inroads. Here America
became the only goal of those seeking an improvement of their
living conditions. While it is difficult to give an accurate picture
of the relationship between internal migration and emigration to
America, there is much to indicate that the 1880s were the only
years in which emigration from certain areas exceeded movement within Sweden.

The economic background of emigration from the Swedish
countryside meant that this movement was highly sensitive to
business cycles, and in both the agricultural and industrial sectors of the national economy. Periods of recession in Swedish
industry heightened emigration, while the opposite was true
during times of prosperity. This sensitivity to industrial conditions was accentuated during the late 1800s when more and
more industrial workers joined the ranks of emigrants bound for

America. The effect of agricultural business cycles is best illustrated during the 1880s when emigration from Europe as a
whole stood at a high level and Swedish emigration soared to
record peaks. All of this movement reflected the impact of price
crashes on the European grain market. As time wore on and
these international contacts increased, the role of fluctuating
business cycles on both sides of the Atlantic assumed greater
importance. Each economic recession in America that did not
carry over to Sweden led to an immediate decline in emigration.
This was the case in the 1870s and again in 1885 and 1892.

Crop failures had nearly catastrophic consequences in rural
areas caught between explosive population growth and sluggish
land development. A succession of three crop failures in 1866–
68 made matters even more desperate. The flight from the
countryside swelled to epidemic proportions, giving rise to the
first mass emigration wave of 1868–69. On the whole, however,
famine and destitution were rarely the direct cause of Swedish
emigration, especially when compared with the situation in such
countries as Ireland. What did have an impact on emigration was
the general fear that crisis conditions would develop and the
belief that too little progress was being made in Sweden to
improve the lot of the agricultural proletariat. Many felt that the
Swedish economy was excessively sluggish, if not stagnant, and
their views were shared by returning emigrants as well as those
who stayed in America and sent back glowing reports of land and
job opportunities.

An even greater impetus to emigration was the impatience of
industrial labor with Swedish conditions. As a rule, this economic
sector held the promise of rapid wage increases and better living
standards. When this trend halted temporarily, many workers
felt they could not wait for better times and, instead, chose to
emigrate. The emigration wave from 1891 to 1893 marked a
turning point in the development of Swedish emigration, as it
began to assume more of the character of an industrial and
urban movement. By this time the supply of prime farmland in
the United States was nearing exhaustion, which dampened the
enthusiasm for emigration among Swedish farmers who worked
their own land or rented from others. With the ebb of group

emigration came the emergence of a new emigrant category dominated by job seekers who made the journey on their own. Although some of them still came from rural areas—farmers' sons, farm hands, maid servants, and the children of small cottagers—increasing numbers were workers in urban industry, crafts, and domestic service. The flight from the Swedish countryside had become a march on the American job market.

The Religious Revival and Temperance Movements

As long as I could swear, dance, drink a bit, and get good marks from the local priest—which I always did—I won the praise of their lordly eminences. But once I renounced my sinful life and accepted Christ into my heart, with the Bible as the rule for my life and conduct, I was threatened with a prison sentence of bread and water. Thousands have gone into voluntary exile because of the un-Christian intolerance and persecuting zeal of the Swedish priesthood.

A Södermanland resident who emigrated
to Minnesota in 1882.[3]

The historical background to these remarks dates all the way back to 1726, when the Conventicle Act was passed prohibiting all religious assemblies ("conventicles") outside the state church. This act was originally aimed against the Pietist movement in eighteenth-century Sweden, but during the first half of the 1800s—at a time of widespread revivalist feeling—it became a symbol for the sovereign authority of the state church. The Pietists, or *läsarna* as they were called, were particularly embittered by the state church and continued to oppose the Conventicle Act by holding devotional meetings in private homes. In their opinion the state church had fallen prey to formalism and secularization, whereas they sought a reawakening of Swedish church life through conversion and the personal religious experience. Lay preachers emerged from their ranks, and some groups organized their own free churches. The Erik Janssonists provide one example, although theirs was a very extreme sect. Other revivalists joined existing free churches, primarily of

Anglo-Saxon origin, such as the Baptists, Mormons, and Methodists.

The Conventicle Act was repealed in 1858, and with that religious intolerance should have disappeared. It would take a long time, however, before the Pietists and their followers were accorded equal status with the state church, and therefore they still considered themselves the object of official persecution. This explains why religious intolerance has often been cited as an important factor in the development of Swedish emigration.

It is often difficult to isolate one particular reason why people emigrated, and it is equally difficult to isolate the religious factor from all the others. The Erik Janssonists offer probably the clearest example of emigration caused by religious intolerance or outright persecution. But looking at the background of subsequent emigration by the Hälsingland dissenters, it becomes clear that the vision of religious freedom in America was only a part of the overall picture. Equally important were the encouraging reports from the Bishop Hill Colony, the New Jerusalem on the Illinois prairie. Religious intolerance functioned only as a contributing factor in the development of Swedish emigration. Its greatest impact was felt during this early period.

If the tensions between the Swedish state church and the free churches were not a significant propellant of Swedish emigration, the American revivalist movements gradually assumed significance as an attractive force. The spread of these movements to Sweden during the 1850s and 1860s enhanced the stature of the mother churches in the eyes of prospective emigrants. American missionaries and a steady stream of religious literature became important carriers of emigration propaganda. Emigrant free-church members wrote letters filled with enthusiastic descriptions of the new country. Their readers from the same small sect—and these sects followed a practice of collective decision making—were especially attracted. Free-church groups throughout Sweden began to think of emigration in the same terms as they thought of the devotional meetings, which brightened an otherwise drab and impoverished life. Emigration became a natural extension of the village path leading to the prayer chapel. This, then, can be called the prime contribution of the revivalist movement to the development of emigration. Many more Swedes emigrated because of the religious freedom associated with the free-church movement than because of the religious intolerance of the state church.

The bonds of unity among free-church groups, which often set them apart from their surroundings, stimulated a spirit of enthusiasm and simplified the tasks of their leadership. The free-church pastor was not only a spiritual leader but in some cases was also a trail-blazer on the uncertain journey to the new and religiously liberal continent on the other side of the Atlantic. It was no coincidence that American promoters of the migrant traffic often turned to free-church pastors in their search for emigrant agents. It is also clear that the American free churches regarded their Swedish brethren as potential emigrants and new members. Confirmation of this comes from the Swedish Baptist, Wilhelm Lindblom, in his report from the American Baptist Convention held in Denver, Colorado, in 1893. During the debate on funds for the Baptist mission in Sweden, Lindblom voiced the opinion that this missionary enterprise could be seen as the groundbreaking for work in America. He was told that this had long been the intention of his "American brethren."[4]

Despite these transatlantic influences, the free-church movement had only a limited impact on Swedish emigration. The very fact that free-church groups existed in certain areas was no guarantee of high emigration rates. While Jönköpings *län* in central Småland might seem an exception to this, economic factors there weighed heavily in the balance. The same is also true of provinces such as Halland, Dalsland, Värmland, and Öland, which were heavily affected by emigration but were not what one would call typical free-church districts.

The American Mormons waged an active emigration campaign that aroused considerable attention during the 1800s. As a rule, conversion to the Mormon faith also implied a decision to emigrate. Copenhagen became the center of these activities in 1850, and of all the Scandinavian countries, Denmark scored the greatest triumphs for the Mormons. The roughly seventeen thousand Danes who emigrated to Utah emerged as the second largest nationality in that state, after the English. Because of its proximity to Denmark, southern Sweden was more affected by the Mormons' activities than other parts of the country. In the early 1900s a special state commission investigated their developments but found that the Mormons had met with limited success in Sweden. It also denied the reports of a white slave trade growing out of the Mormons' polygamist practices. All in all, some seventy-five hundred Mormons emigrated from Sweden.

The temperance movement often went hand-in-hand with the free-church movement and has sometimes been regarded as an important factor in the development of mass emigration. If official intolerance of temperance activities had any affect on emigration, it was probably limited to certain priests in the state church. Many people were opposed to the movement because of its restrictions on personal freedom, and this was made clear to several temperance-minded clergymen when they failed to secure appointments to state Lutheran congregations. Their deep-rooted convictions set them at odds with the church authorities who, while finding no fault with the movement as such, saw this unofficial involvement by state clergymen as a show of opposition and flagging loyalty. Some of these priests eventually emigrated to America, and one of them, Lars Paul Esbjörn, later assumed a leading position in the Augustana Synod. What has been said of the free churches also applies to the temperance movement: its greatest impact on emigration stemmed from the contacts it had in America, which was the birthplace of the Swedish temperance movement.

Class Differences

Han ville bort till det stora landet i väster,
där ingen kung finns och inga kitsliga präster.
Där man får sova och äta fläsk och potatis
och så med flottet kan smörja stövlarna gratis.

Där ingen länsman törs stöta bonden för pannan
och renat brännvin kan fås för sex styver kannan.

His dream was to sail to that land out west,
where no kings or priests rule one's life as a pest.
Where a man can find ease, fill his stomach to the core,

and grease his boots free with the fat of a boar.
Where a sheriff thinks twice, if a farmer he'll throttle
and good *snaps* can be had for six cents to the bottle.
From "Petter Jönssons Resa till Amerika."[5]

Here we have rich men, here we have learned men, here
we have smart men, here we have bosses who sometimes work
us like dogs—but *masters* we have none.
A Småland resident who emigrated to America in 1868.[6]

Emigrant ballads and Swedish-American folklore frequently portray the social injustices of nineteenth-century Sweden as important causes of emigration. The question can be raised, however, whether this picture of Swedish society was more a product of emigration propaganda than a reflection of actual fact. This does not mean that Sweden was without its share of social restrictions, stodgy class mentality, and bureaucratic management, but there is a great deal of evidence that the popular reaction to these conditions could not have stimulated emigration without the corresponding vision of America as a country where all men were equals.

It is true that the Swedish lower classes harbored feelings of inferiority that sometimes gave rise to resentment and hatred toward the upper, ruling classes. It is also true, however, that this lower-class consciousness lacked both a strong sense of class solidarity and a conviction that class struggle was inevitable. The situation in Sweden mirrored conditions throughout Europe. An open show of protest against established society was generally considered unnecessary; thus social injustice alone did not create a need to emigrate.

As they learned more about working conditions in the United States, Swedes began to realize that slums and class differences were not limited to Sweden. The Swedish labor movement, which was growing at the time, no longer regarded America as the promised land, but rather as the domain of ruthless financiers and private capital. One thing, however, fascinated Swedish workers, even though it never became an independent stimulus of emigration—the fact that American workers were not treated as an inferior class. As time went by, a growing awareness of American social norms and group behavior gave Swedes the impression that Americans had no masters but themselves.

The class structure of nineteenth-century Swedish society was responsible for another emigration factor, and one that perhaps was just as important. Swedes saw that the possibilities of moving up on the social ladder were greater in America than at home. Visiting Swedish Americans almost always were irritated by the indifference of the Swedish poor to their own situation and its improvement.

A final emigration factor with social-class overtones stems from the prevailing economic conditions in the Swedish countryside. The shortage of farm acreage forced many farmers' sons to find work on other farms, in urban industries, or with the railroad teams in northern Sweden. In the process of becoming wage earners, they dropped to a lower social standing than they were accustomed to. This led to feelings of discontent—feelings that disappeared as soon as they had emigrated and started a new life as independent farmers. Around the turn of the century a crown sheriff in Dalsland described the situation in these words: "The sons and daughters of fairly wealthy farmers are emigrating instead of finding work in Swedish cities. Why? Because in Sweden at least it is still beneath the dignity and standards of the farming aristocracy to join up with the working masses and their socialistic tendencies."[7]

Political Immaturity

The political immaturity of the period drove me here. . . .
Here everyone is entitled to his full share, is of legal age, and has the vote at twenty-one. . . . If he is a citizen he has the right to seek public office.
The comments of a Värmland emigrant in 1905.[8]

On the surface, at least, the lack of political freedom in Sweden looms as a significant factor in the development of mass emigration. The vast majority of emigrants had no representation in the Swedish Parliament and therefore had little political influence. Although the old Estates Parliament was abolished in 1866, two years before the start of mass emigration, the reform meant little to the rural and urban working class. The introduction of voting age requirements gave the ballot to only 20 percent of all men of legal age; the working class was left out entirely. The next voting reforms came in 1909, when 75 percent of all adult males obtained the right to vote. By this time, when emigration had started to decline, a combination of higher wages and general inflation enabled the working class to overcome the economic obstacles to the ballot box, despite the absence of political reform. In 1909 the Social Democratic party gained thirty-four representatives in the Second Chamber of Parliament. In 1918, when emigration had ceased to be a mass phenomenon, almost all of the adult population had won the right to vote. The democratic breakthrough was a reality in Sweden.

The apparent relationship between the decline of emigration and the extension of voting rights is only that—apparent and misleading. Although the majority of emigrants must have been dissatisfied with the political situation, their feelings cannot have had any singular impact on their decision to leave the country. True, Swedish Americans often say that the absence of voting reforms was one of the reasons they emigrated. American interests in the migrant traffic also helped things along by headlining the vision of universal suffrage in the United States. The radical Swedish press, however, played the most important role in linking emigration to political dissent. According to these newspapers and the radical political factions that advocated sweeping voting reforms, emigration provided an altogether appropriate means of protesting the injustices in Swedish society. The political columns of the radical press were filled with contributions from visiting Swedish Americans which ran under the title of "Testimonies on Behalf of Universal Suffrage." As a result, emigration and political dissent became largely synonymous, regardless of whether the individual emigrant had any real feelings on the matter.

After the 1880s larger numbers of Swedish workers booked passage on emigrant ships. In their letters home they described the uneven struggle of the trade unions against American capital and industrial finance. The increasingly negative reports from this bastion of universal suffrage probably dampened the feelings of political dissatisfaction among Swedish workers. The following comments from one Swedish American are not entirely unique in this respect: "Universal suffrage is a fine thing if you take advantage of your own right to vote. But most people sell their votes for something between five and ten cents and let the moneyman do what he thinks is best. The millionaire has the poor wrapped around his little finger. You can't buy or sell anything he hasn't already put a price on."[9] A study of the political background of mass emigration reinforces the observation that oppression, in whatever shape or form, had no central impact on Swedish developments. The ultimate factor was the desire people had to improve their living standards.

Military Service

> Poor wages were not the only reason I left Sweden. The long period of military service haunted me like a ghost and gave a dark outlook to the future.
> A Jämtland resident who emigrated in 1905.

> No, I love my country even more today, but it was the long stint of military service that made me emigrate. I had no desire to train that long, and there are a lot of others here who say the same.

> I did my military service before I emigrated. But I have two young boys, and I'm going to see to it that they don't end up in a school for murderers.
> The comments of emigrants from 1903.[10]

Throughout the period of mass Swedish migration a royal decree prohibited the emigration of military conscripts unless they had special permission. Up to 1840 all emigration from Sweden was illegal, but once this general ban was lifted the decree affecting military conscripts remained the primary legal obstacle to emigration. As a result, evidence of "draft evasion" among Swedish emigrants became a special topic of concern.

At the beginning of this century the Swedish State Commission on Emigration investigated the matter and, by way of statistics, arrived at the conclusion that there was substantial relationship between emigration and military service. In the commission's view, every extension of military service periods was followed by a temporary increase of emigration by twenty-year olds, or men who were next in line for induction. In 1866, when recruits spent thirty days in training, twenty-year olds made up approximately 4 percent of all male emigrants. In 1909, when the training period was 240 days, this figure stood approximately 17 percent.

Methods of processing applications for permission to emigrate varied considerably during this period, but for many years nearly every single applicant was granted permission. Toward the end of the 1800s, however, stricter procedures were introduced, and as a rule permits were issued only to those who had completed their service periods. Men who had reached the age of induction and had not received royal permission to emigrate could not be issued migration certificates. According to a law passed in 1884, such a certificate was required of every conscript who booked passage with emigrant agents. Failure to display such a certificate meant that conscripts could not even buy a steamship ticket for America. By contracting with non-Swedish agents, however, emigrants could circumvent these regulations.

The 1884 legislation led to illegal emigration, primarily by way of Copenhagen but also from the Norwegian ports of Trondheim and Oslo. Since Danish and Norwegian agents were not bound by Swedish regulations, they became the focus of black market emigrant operations. Here emigrants could purchase counterfeit migration certificates and other necessary documents, which were often concealed in the famous "America vests." There is also evidence that black market agents were not charging inflated prices for their services. In 1909, for example, a customs officer in Skane reported to the Swedish emigration commission that "there are some places in Copenhagen where emigrants can obtain a complete set of papers for only fifty *öre* (about ten cents). Similar purchases could be made, he added, "in a certain Malmö shop," which offered emigrants an enticing addition to their traveling wardrobes—"a vest with a pocket containing a counterfeit migration certificate."[11]

Evasion of military service was not unusual; in fact it even had the character of a well-publicized secret. This is illustrated by an interview made in Jamestown, Pennsylvania, with a Swede who emigrated with a companion from a forest in Halland province in 1913. During the train ride to the provincial capital of Halmstad, the two young men happened to bump into the district sheriff, who asked where they were headed. "To Halmstad," they replied. "Come on now," said the sheriff. "I can see that you're on your way to America. Listen, if you're running away from military service you've got it all wrong. There's nothing to be afraid of. Stay at home." The sheriff ended the conversation by saying: "Give my regards to Copenhagen and New York when you get there."[12]

In studying the causes of emigration, research has led to the conclusion that opposition to military service, like all other noneconomic factors, was not of decisive importance. On the other hand, the threat of military service did have significance in the decision-making process behind emigration when young men were considering the pros and cons of staying in Sweden and the prospects of a new start in America. Those who emigrated for economic reasons often made plans to leave the country near the time of induction. In other words, it was not the fear of military service itself but rather the timing of induction that caused many young men to emigrate.

Historians also have questioned the reasoning of the Swedish emigration commission, which saw a direct connection between increased emigration and extended periods of military service. It is true that emigration by twenty-year olds increased both in 1887 and 1902, when decisions were made to lengthen military training periods. On the other hand, this emigration declined in 1893 and 1894, immediately after the training period had been extended for forty-two to ninety-two days. The official emigration statistics, then, do not give historians any clear trend to go by. At the same time it is likely that illegal or unauthorized emigration by way of foreign ports increased when training periods were lengthened or when the issuance of royal permits became more restrictive.

In general, the lower classes of Swedish society did not look upon military service with any great favor, which is one reason why it assumes significance as a push factor of emigration to America. There is also evidence that class differences lay behind this disfavor. In 1857 the period of military service was a maximum of 30 days; in 1885, 45 days; in 1892, 90 days; and in 1901, 240 days. Today these training periods seem relatively humane, and military service is something we expect in a modern democracy. Most young Swedes during the 1800s and early 1900s, however, regarded military service as an intrusion on their personal freedoms. For many of them it was the epitome of humiliation, symbolizing the utter destitution of the poor and the oppression of the ruling classes. In 1913 one military officer bent on reform characterized the situation in these terms:

> An officer takes no pains to win people to his authority or the cause of his country. He couldn't care less about teaching conscripts the necessity of military service, the meaning and purpose of all the details, the rules of discipline, the need for force, and the subjugation of all individuals to a code of authority. He merely presumes that people understand all of this. An officer acts only with these principles in mind: command with authority; never take back an order; allow for no deviations or discussion, even if the command was incorrect, for that is damaging to both prestige and discipline![13]

A trainee from Jösse *härad* in Värmland shared the same feelings:

> It is easy to understand why young people are leaving for America. When I was in the service—last year was my final stint—there was nothing in the world I regretted more than I hadn't emigrated myself. Military training was the worst thing I had ever experienced, and I often wondered what I had ever done to deserve such punishment. When the trainees at Trossnäs come home and tell their stories, it's perfectly clear

why men who are awaiting induction are trying to get out of it
by leaving the country.[14]

The negative side of military training found its way into
stories, which were told and retold in much the same way as the
tales of the American West. In their own way they contributed
something to the total emigration picture. As a Jämtland emigrant explained in 1905: "Some friends of mine told me that
once you were out on the training field you were called everything from blooming idiot and scoundrel to crackpot and
louse—not to mention the more indecent variety. If I had to put
up with that kind of name-calling I didn't want any part of it."[15]

Improved Communications

The completion of this railroad line has dealt a major blow
to the worst enemy of our civilization—distances. We can
now begin to call ourselves true Europeans. Our travels are no
longer being measured in Asiatic fashion, by number of days
or marches between encampments, but rather by minutes and
hours.

Newspaper commentary on the inauguration
of the West Swedish railroad line in 1862.

This well-known Atlantic Steamship Company, whose ships
boast the most up-to-date accommodations for the comfort
of their passengers, is the only one to offer emigrants special
first-class passage on the steamships *Scandinavia* and *Scotia*.

Advertisement for the Anchor Line, 1870.

Two developments simplified the emigration process and
made the transatlantic journey far more attractive, both in terms
of safety and economics. One was the expansion of the Swedish
railroad network during the 1860s; the other, the introduction
of safer and cheaper means of transatlantic travel.

"If the Swedish railroads had been built twenty years earlier
emigration would have been stopped." There is some truth to
this statement, as the coming of the railroads created new con-

struction jobs and opened new possibilities for remote villages and entire districts. On the other hand, mass emigration from Sweden could hardly have materialized without direct lines of communication between emigrants' home districts and ports of embarkation. Some emigration researchers also claim that the late development of the Swedish railroad network explains the delay in the start of mass emigration from Sweden as compared with the rest of northern Europe. It was not until 1862 that Stockholm was linked to the western port city of Gothenburg. Two years later a southern line was opened between Malmö, Falköping, and Stockholm.

Although the railroads reduced the cost and difficulties of transportation in Sweden, they did not solve all of the problems facing Swedish emigrants. The Atlantic crossing was still a major hurdle, but changes took place during the 1860s that ultimately paved the way for mass emigration. The long and often hazardous journey by Swedish and American sailing vessels to East Coast ports was replaced by inexpensive and relatively trouble-free passage on large steamships operated by major shipping lines. The experiences emigrants had on board these ships are worth a chapter in themselves. Something should be said at this point, however, about ticket prices for transatlantic travel.

Business competition between Atlantic shipping lines caused considerable fluctuations in ticket prices throughout the mass-emigration era. In general, passage from Gothenburg to New York or, as was more often the case, Gothenburg to Chicago, was very cheap. In 1869, for example, a one-way ticket from Gothenburg to Chicago cost approximately 165 *riksdaler* (about $41); during the 1880s, approximately 105 crowns (about $28); and at the beginning of the 1900s, approximately 175 crowns (about $47). These were the official prices, but in reality they were often lower due to business competition.

What did this mean, then, in terms of emigrants' buying power? Wages, of course, were low in Sweden at this time: aside from free food and lodgings, a farm-hand could count on an annual income of 100 crowns ($27) in 1869; 138 crowns (about $37) during the 1880s; and 222 crowns (about $60) at the beginning of this century. Around 1870 a Swedish railroad worker

earned an average of 1.5 crowns ($.40) per day, excluding food
and lodging. Within a reasonable length of time, however, either
of the two could save enough for an emigrant-class steamship
ticket. Because of the higher wage scales and advantageous
exchange rates it was even easier for friends and relatives in
America to purchase tickets ahead of time and forward them to
Sweden.

While the American railroads simplified travel from the port
cities on the eastern seaboard to the farms of the Middle West,
they did not have any major effect on the development of
Swedish emigration. Railroad construction had reached the Mississippi Valley as early as the 1850s, even before the start of mass
Swedish emigration. Those who came earlier had little problem
reaching their destinations, either by river and canal boat,
stagecoach and carriage, or on foot. The feeling seemed to be
that once a person had arrived on the American side, everything
would take care of itself.

News of America in the Swedish Press

On the whole, and especially up to World War I, the Swedish
press was strongly opposed to emigration. Newspaper editorials
denounced the exodus and branded all emigrants as traitors.
Small news items describing the plight of emigrants in America
were inserted on the regular news pages in an effort to discour-
age further emigration. The only exceptions to this journalism
were several radical newspapers that regarded emigration as a
suitable means of protesting all of the injustices in Swedish
society. In the long run the position taken by most of the Swedish
press was self-defeating: it only heightened the America fever
among the Swedish population.

Had they placed a ban on all news from America and Swedish
immigrant settlements, these newspapers might have put a stop
to emigration. Instead, their enormous coverage of developments on the other side of the Atlantic revitalized the
image of the New World and made it more familiar to thousands
of readers. A regular feature of most major papers was the
"Letters from America" columns, in which special correspon-

dents or Swedish Americans reported on immigrant living conditions. At times whole articles were reprinted from leading
Swedish-American newspapers, such as *Hemlandet* and *Svenska
Amerikanaren,* and the advertizing sections were swamped with
the glowing accounts of emigrant agents' operations. When one
considers all of these factors it becomes clear that the viewpoints
expressed on the editorial pages carried very little weight.

Nearly all of the conditions held responsible for the development of Swedish emigration have one thing in common.
Although each of them had a role to play in this transatlantic
movement, none had any singular importance for the overall
picture. As a whole, the only factors that induced people to
emigrate were economic.

Distribution of Emigration in Sweden

Figures 3 and 4 show the differences in the start and spread
of emigration throughout Sweden. Emigration intensity was
highest in the following six *län* or administrative districts: Halland, Jönköping, Värmland, Kronoberg, Kalmar, and Älvsborg.
Together with western Älvsborg, southwestern Östergötland,
Kopparberg, and western Örebro *län,* these six districts form
one large, interconnecting region which during the mass emigration era represented only 30 percent of the nation's population but accounted for almost half of all Swedish emigrants to
America. If one looks at the old provincial divisions instead of
administrative districts *(län),* however, Öland and Dalsland were
the two small areas hardest hit by emigration.

In rural areas the following push factors had significance for
the development of emigration: the absence of expanding cities
or industrial centers, the lack of prime farmland, and the lack of
new territory for agricultural expansion. Emigration from
urban areas was especially strong in cases where a large percentage of the population originally came from rural areas or where
industries were highly susceptible to changes in economic patterns. One thing was true of both urban and rural areas: if
emigration happened to start early, it usually continued at a high
rate of intensity during the rest of the emigration period.

Figure 3. Total Emigration from the Swedish *län* (administrative districts), 1851–1925.

Nationwide: 1,084,874

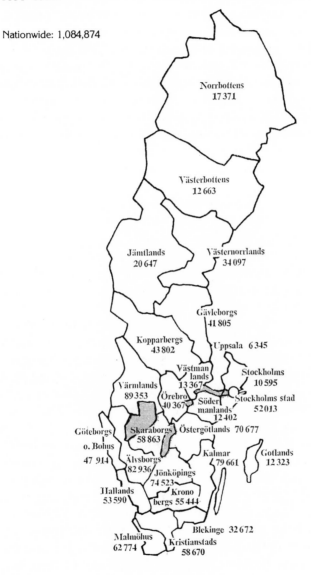

A look at the first three decades of Swedish emigration shows a number of regional differences. During the 1840s and 1850s, southern Östergötland, northern and southern Småland, parts of Blekinge, and northern Skåne were the major areas of emigration. One particular area, which included parts of Hälsingland, eastern Dalarna, and northern Uppland, also experienced high emigration due to the activities of the Erik Janssonists. The crop failures of the 1860s and the start of the mass emigration era enlarged this geographical picture. The older emigrant districts in Småland, Blekinge, and Skåne were joined by central Västergötland and parts of Dalsland, Värmland, Dalarna, and Jämtland, all of which had a high emigration intensity.

These same districts entered into the picture during the peak emigration years of the 1880s, and over the course of one decade more people emigrated from Värmland than from any other part of Sweden, either before or after. The greatest increase in emigration, however, took place in Hallands *län*, with a record average emigration of 12.08 persons per year and per 1,000 residents. Emigration also undercut the normal population growth in Jönköpings, Hallands, Kronobergs, Värmlands, and Älvsborgs *län*. Special centers of emigration developed within each of the leading *län:* in Värmland, the areas along the Dalsland and Norwegian borders as well as the Karlskoga mining district (Örebro *län*); in Dalsland, the central flatland areas and the districts along the Bohuslän border; in Skaraborgs *län*, the southern plains area around Skara and the Fal district; in Älvsborgs *lan*, the area around Ulricehamn and the timberland parishes adjacent to Jönköpings and Hallands *län*; in Jönköpings *län*, the areas around Gränna, Vetlanda, and Sävsjö as well as the parishes bordering along Älvsborgs *län;* in Kronobergs *län*, the Lagan and Helgeån districts. Two distinct emigration districts emerged in Kalmar *län*, one to the north, in the Vimmerby area, and one to the east, the island of Öland, which lost 12 to 13 percent of its population during the 1880s. In Östergötland emigration was heaviest from Holaveden and the southern flatland areas around Vadstena, while in Kristianstads *län* it was concentrated to the Bjäre area and the northern flatland and

Figure 4. Emigration from the Swedish *län* in Relationship to Population, 1881–1890.

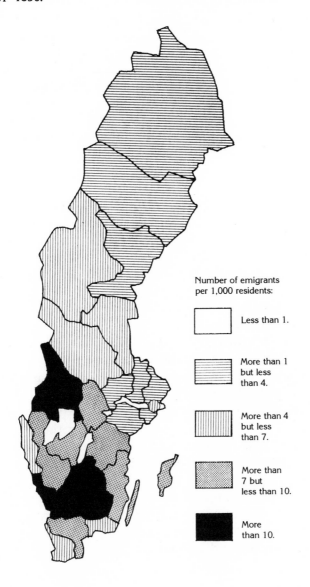

Number of emigrants per 1,000 residents:

Less than 1.

More than 1 but less than 4.

More than 4 but less than 7.

More than 7 but less than 10.

More than 10.

timber districts. In Hallands *län,* however, nearly all districts had the same high level of emigration.

From 1890 to 1910 the older emigrant districts in Småland began to lose some of their importance, even though they still ranked high in the statistical columns. Kalmar *län,* in particular, experienced heavy emigration during this twenty-year period and ranked third, behind Värmlands and Älvsborgs *län* in terms of absolute statistics, i.e. the total number of emigrants. Emigration from Hallands *län* was higher, however, when seen in terms of relative statistics, i.e. the number of emigrants relative to the population. Of all the older emigrant districts, Östergötlands *län* experienced the most rapid decline of emigration during this period. Otherwise, the major change between 1890 and 1910 was the increased emigration from the Stockholm area and the northern Swedish districts. The Stockholm statistics reflect the migration surge among the industrial working class. Compared with developments in most of central and southern Sweden, emigration from northern Sweden peaked rather late, reaching record heights in all districts between 1901 and 1910. In fact, one-fifth of the nation's emigrants came from northern Sweden during this decade.

Although World War I had a dampening affect on emigration from 1911 to 1920, it did not completely halt movement from any single district in Sweden. Värmland retained the lead in the statistical columns, followed closely by Kälmar *lan.* Emigration was also high along the Swedish West Coast, and Älvsborgs *län* maintained its position among the leaders. The same was also true for the city of Stockholm and, especially, for the northern Swedish districts, which accounted for one-seventh of the nation's emigrants.

The same geographical picture characterized the last five years of mass emigration from 1920 to 1925. In terms of absolute figures, however, Kopparbergs *län* took a third-place ranking behind Värmlands and Kalmar *län.*

4   America for Sale

Two sets of factors were responsible for the development of mass emigration. First were the push factors, represented by the deplorable conditions in nineteenth- and early twentieth-century Swedish society. The second were the pull factors, the dreams and promises that America had to offer and that were made even more attractive to European eyes by those who "sold America." The most significant pull factors were land and job opportunities along with the transportation possibilities that made these dreams and promises a reality. The chief promoters of emigration to the United States were the federal government, local and state authorities, major land companies, American industry, railroads, Atlantic steamship lines, and, last but not least, Swedish Americans themselves.

Cheap Land on Convenient Terms

In the early 1800s America was still a very young nation with a gigantic surplus of unsettled land. By the time mass emigration began from Sweden, the American frontier had reached the Mississippi Valley. East of this frontier there was still private land for sale, but the asking price was usually more than a poor emigrant could afford. Up until 1890, then, the primary goals of land-hungry Swedes were the government-land holdings along the frontier or farther west.

The management and sale of government land were spelled

51

out in two pieces of legislation, each of which set the stage for new settlement. The first of these came in 1841 and coincided with the start of group emigration from Sweden. The Preemption Law stipulated that government land was to be sold at a cheap and stable price, $1.25 per acre. Up to that time government land had been sold as auction lots. The second piece of legislation, the Homestead Act, came in 1862, just before mass emigration began from Sweden. This legislation offered 160 acres of free land to any American citizen of legal age or any immigrant who had notified the government of his decision to become a citizen. Those who worked and lived on the land for five years were entitled to full ownership, but this offer would be made only once. The purpose of the Homestead Act was to attract new settlers to the vast territory west of the Mississippi; it had enormous significance for European immigrants, particularly poor and land-hungry Scandinavians. Homestead land was available from the late 1860s up to around 1890, years which marked the beginning and end of peak emigration from Sweden. Even today most of the larger Swedish settlements can be found in the Homestead Triangle between the upper reaches of the Mississippi and Missouri Rivers.

Free government land was usually located in remote wilderness regions, and therefore it did not hold the same attraction for all newcomers. Those who arrived in this country with investment capital—the Swedish farmers, for example, who sold their homes and property—saw the advantages of buying private land in more populated areas. Here they found a ready supply of sellers and speculators. Some sellers were early pioneers who had either bought or taken government land and who wanted to make a profit on their holdings now that the frontier had pushed farther west. Others were land speculators and land companies who bought vast amounts of acreage for the same purpose. By far the most important sellers to Swedish immigrants were the railroad companies, which had been given land by the government to finance railroad construction.

How much, then, did emigrants have to pay for this land? That is a difficult question to answer, mainly because conditions changed so rapidly across the country. In general, however, the major land companies and the railroads kept prices low and well within the reach of Swedish emigrants, while private homesteaders and fairly settled farmers followed a price scale roughly comparable to conditions on the Swedish market. Actually, it was only a question of time before an emigrant who had arrived in this country without ready cash could save enough to invest in a good-sized farm. There were two reasons for this. First, if he bought land from one of the larger companies he could usually make payments over a period of eight full years. Second, job opportunities and wages were so favorable that it was comparatively easy to set aside the required capital. Although soil quality varied from one part of the country to the other, it was generally richer and more productive than the soil immigrants were accustomed to in Sweden. This was especially true out on the prairie, although Swedes were at first very sceptical of open farming and assumed that if there were no trees in sight there was something wrong with the soil.

Good Wages, Plenty of Jobs

America's job opportunities provided the second major attraction for Swedish immigrants. After the Civil War, the economic growth of the northern and eastern states opened a wide range of new jobs and employment opportunities. The start of mass Swedish emigration coincided with the demand for skilled and unskilled labor from the eastern seaboard to the plains of the Middle West. The eastern states were primarily interested in industrial labor and better skilled hands, while the Middle West attracted farmhands, lumberjacks, railroad workers, and unskilled labor. These conditions also meant that the wage scale for unskilled labor was considerably higher in the Middle West than it was in the East. Prior to 1890 most Swedish immigrants got their start in the Middle West as lumberjacks, farm hands, railroad workers, or domestics. The rest found places to stay with friends or relatives in eastern cities or took jobs in the factories and private homes in cities such as Chicago and Minneapolis.

After 1890 things began to change. The Swedish settlements in the Middle West emerged from the primitiveness of frontier life, but continued to attract new immigrants. Here there was still a need for farm workers and domestics. Railroad teams and lumberjacks, however, pushed westward, as far as their jobs would take them, while a larger share of unskilled Swedish labor took jobs in factories and public service. The industrial working class began its march on the American job market, settling primarily in the industrial cities along the eastern seaboard.

In the beginning it was not the surplus of job opportunities that attracted these newcomers but rather the prospect of higher wages. Work was not scarce in Sweden, and unemployment was not a major threat during the mass emigration era. Those who made their way to the Middle West found a crying need for unskilled labor, which had sent wage levels spiraling. A farm hand in America could earn two to three times as much per year as he could in Sweden, and the prospects were even better for skilled laborers such as carpenters and blacksmiths. Unskilled labor also drew the benefit of a staggered pay scale, where earnings fluctuated with the seasons of the year. This was not the case in Sweden. While a Minnesota farm hand earned between thirty-five and seventy cents per day in June of 1867, he could count on making four dollars a day during harvest seasons, two months later. One can well imagine how this news was received in Sweden, where farm hands earned only about thirty cents a day.

In general, American industrial wages were much higher than Swedish wages. After 1900, however, the American labor market lost its appeal among the Swedish working classes which, in contrast to earlier emigrants, had closer ties to urban and industrial environments. As labor-market conditions hardened, emigrants began to see the difference between the conservative flavor of the American business world and the liberal-minded outlook of Europe's industrialized nations. Writing home from cities such as New York, Chicago, Philadelphia, and Boston, emigrants began to criticize the incessant demand for production, the hard-nosed business competition, the widespread corruption, and the helpless situation of the trade unions.

From the 1860s to the 1890s, the prime objective of Swedish immigrants was to own their own farms. What made it possible for them to make payments on their land and meet the initial requirements of a homestead farmer was the ready supply of jobs on the American labor market. As a rule, a homesteader had to invest approximately one thousand dollars before his farm began to produce enough to sustain an entire household. The Homestead Act made provisions for this by allowing home-steaders to work away from their farms for periods of up to six months during each of the first five years. Those who used this option ran no risk of losing title to their lands. During the fall and winter months, many Swedish homesteaders found work as lumberjacks and miners, or helped build the western railroads. In this respect, then, the Homestead Triangle provided an ideal setting for the immigrant worker.

Convenient Transportation Routes

America offered the newcomer three basic transportation routes. The first two went west, bringing him into contact with job opportunities and homestead land, while the third went east and determined the value of new farm acreage. Once emigrants had crossed the Atlantic, the eastern port cities were their first important transit stations on the road west. During the 1850s the American railroads gained control of this transportation route, and by the end of the same decade immigrants could travel by rail as far west as the Mississippi. Ten years later the railroads had crossed the Mississippi, carrying more passengers than the combined total on stagecoaches and steamboats. For a long time to come, however, immigrants would have to blaze their own trails to isolated land sections or distant lumber camps.

Although emigrants were more concerned about transporta-tion costs than passenger comfort, they publicized their com-plaints about the conditions on board Atlantic steamships and emigrant trains, taking some revenge on company reputations on both sides of the Atlantic. On the whole, emigrant-class pas-sengers enjoyed the same comforts, or lack of comforts, regard-less of whether they traveled by boat or train. Even the name of the company was immaterial. What was important was the cost of transportation, which at times was determined by secret concessions and gentlemen's agreements among interests in the emigrant traffic. At other times price wars kept costs to a bare minimum and, for that reason, can almost be said to have encouraged emigration.

Transcontinental railroads formed an integral link between the farms of the Middle West and their markets to the east. Without them the homestead lands would have had little economic value, and farmers would not have had the slightest hope of selling their produce. New lines of track were being built, and they pushed deep into the frontier west of the Mississippi, joining farms and homesteads with the main lines to the east. This transportation network was to have special significance for Swedish emigrants, as it offered them the full range of opportunities on the American continent—communications, land, and jobs.

America and its opportunities found a ready corps of "salesmen," who welcomed the first immigrants with open arms and did everything in their power to encourage others to follow. Emigration became a highly diversified business, where competition ran as high as the sales prospects. The term "emigration industry" is a fitting description of the ways in which these business interests helped sell America to new emigrants.

5 They Sold America

The Federal and State Governments

It was only natural that the federal government took an interest in the emigrant traffic. America was a large continent that could be populated only with help from other shores. This was the thrust of the liberal immigration legislation up to World War I. The federal government also took an active role in selling America, primarily through the passage of the Homestead Act with its offer of free government land. Of somewhat lesser importance were the import laws of 1861–65, affecting contract emigrant labor. This legislation entitled American industry to import European workers on the condition that they repaid their travel costs through work in this country. The privately-owned American Emigrant Company was established as a partner in this scheme, but the whole affair failed to live up to expectations. Aside from purely practical problems, there was strident opposition from workers, and by 1885 the import traffic had lost so much public favor that it was outlawed entirely.

On the other hand, the federal government did not wage any major propaganda campaign in support of emigration. Although the American consulates in such cities as Gothenburg and Stockholm became hotbeds of emigration activity during the 1860s, the Stockholm legation had been instructed by Washington to proceed with caution and, at all costs, to avoid irritating the antiemigration sentiments of the Swedish government. The

difference between the activities of the American consuls and
the viewpoints of the federal government are spelled out in two
documents from this period. The report of the American consul
in Stockholm for 1868 contained the following words: "During
the past winter I was occupied in organizing individually a
Swedish Emigration Company, which is in full vigor at present."[1]
Three years later the American minister in Stockholm received
the following instructions from his superiors in Washington:
"You will, of course, be careful to publish nothing over your own
signature."[2]

Meanwhile, emigration was receiving encouragement from
various state governments, particularly in and around the
Upper Mississippi Valley where the opening of homestead lands
and new frontier settlements attracted scores of northern European immigrants. Before the Civil War the southern states had
been relatively untouched by immigration, but during the Re-
construction era some of them made an effort to win a share of
this new settlement wave. Regardless of its geography, each state
had two basic interests at stake in the campaign for new settlers
and industrial capital: the exploitation of its own natural resources and the stimulation of its economy to levels reached by
states farther east. Neither objective could be attained without
the help of private industry and major land companies, and
from the 1880s on most of these sales operations were handled
by private interests. Immigration policies were another matter,
however, and during the ten to fifteen years after the Civil War,
state governments took an active hand in planning for the future. During this time, newly settled immigrant groups made
their own contributions. Minnesota offers a striking example of
this, particularly from the standpoint of Swedish-American interests.

For Sale: Minnesota

Even before the Civil War, the state of Minnesota had made
its way into the advertising sections of the leading American
newspapers and, through well-placed agents, into the eastern
port cities. After 1865 the search for new settlers increased at a

rapid pace. A contest was arranged to determine the best advertising brochure for the whole state, with the winning proposal to be published in English, German, and Norwegian and distributed by the general population. Minnesota residents were asked to submit the names and addresses of persons in the United States or Europe who might be interested in receiving a copy of the brochure. The decision to print the winning proposal in Norwegian was a practical one and was not meant to exclude the Swedish population. The only Scandinavian printing press in the Upper Mississippi Valley at the time belonged to a Norwegian newspaper in Madison, Wisconsin, and it was there that the Norwegian edition appeared in 1865. The German version did not appear until 1867, and therefore the Scandinavian population was the only non-English speaking group to receive the first copies of this brochure for distribution at home and abroad.

For decades to come the Norwegian and Swedish populations of Minnesota were to play a special role in the formation of that state's immigration policy. Hans Mattson, formerly a colonel in the Union Army, was instrumental in establishing the Minnesota Board of Immigration in 1867, serving as its secretary and major figure. The prime objectives of the board were emigration propaganda and emigrant protection, both of which relied heavily on the contributions of resident immigrant groups. Mattson himself wrote a brochure for the Scandinavian population, publishing it in Norwegian and Swedish, contributed articles to the Scandinavian-American press, and corresponded with clergymen and other prominent immigrants in the United States. His articles won an immediate response from readers, and at the end of March 1867, Mattson informed the governor of Minnesota that he had no less than 122 letters to answer from all parts of the country.

From the very start most of the board's promotional appeals were directed to Scandinavian Americans. Mattson's own articles in the immigrant press concluded with a standard phrase: "It is my belief that if the Swedish newspapers have any concern for the welfare of their country's emigrants they can perform no better service than to inform those destined for Minnesota of the arrangements our state has made on their behalf." Unfortunately, his appeal did not win sympathy in Sweden, where the newspapers were largely opposed to emigration.

In its brochures as well, the Board of Immigration underlined its interest in attracting Scandinavians from other parts of the Middle West and East. The Swedish brochure carried a rather extensive title: "Minnesota and its advantages for the immigrant, containing a description of the state's history, geography, government, cities, rivers, lakes, forests, climate, soil, minerals, railroads, commerce, industries, etc., which are of interest and importance for those seeking their homes in the West." For the most part the brochure was a factual description of what Minnesota had to offer newcomers. It specifically emphasized the fact that Swedes could carve out a future for themselves in the state as farmers and homesteaders. Land, in other words, was the key to success: other job opportunities would be of help to them only during their first years as settlers.

Emigrant protection was a special concern of Minnesota's Scandinavian population, and for this reason the Board of Immigration stationed a Scandinavian-born agent in four key cities on the North American continent. Their specific responsibilities were to aid new arrivals and encourage them to settle in Minnesota. Two of these agents were stationed in the port cities of New York—where most of the Swedes landed—and Quebec, which was the major port of debarkation for Norwegian immigrants. The others made contacts with new arrivals in the railroad capitals of Chicago and Milwaukee. The large majority of Swedes changed trains in Chicago after the journey from New York, while the Norwegians frequently chose Milwaukee as an in-transit station on the road west. The New York and Quebec agents soon discovered, however, that they could be of little assistance to new immigrants. By the time contacts could be made, immigrants had already purchased their tickets, deposited their baggage, exchanged their currencies, and were ready to leave the city. In New York's Castle Garden, for example, the only persons with authorized access to arriving immigrants were certain well-placed railroad company agents. As as a result, the Minnesota Board of Immigration was forced to concentrate its efforts in Chicago and Milwaukee, where opportunities were far

Portrait of Hans Mattson at the time of his commission as a colonel in the Union Army, 1863.

In the 1860s the English Wilson Line began to shuttle emigrants across the North Sea from Gothenburg to Hull on the first leg of their Journey.

Brigs loaded with iron bars carried the first emigrants across the Atlantic. This model, "Tre Kronor," served also as the model for *"Charlotta,"* on which Karl Oskar and Kristina sailed in Vilhelm Moberg's emigrant novels.

Emigrants en route to the port city of Gothenburg. Painted by
G. Saloman, 1872.

Typical immigrant homes in Chicago's "Swede Town" around 1880.

Swedish lumberjacks at work felling giant California redwoods in 1901.

Homestead in Red River Valley, Minnesota.

Family in front of a sod hut in South Dakota, 1910.

On board an emigrant liner in the 1920s.

The Swedish American Line's first passenger liner, *"Stockholm."*

more promising. Regardless of where immigrants had purchased their train tickets—in Sweden, New York, or Quebec—all
roads converged on these two middle western cities. Those destined for points farther west were once again confronted with
the problems of travel itineraries, ticket purchases, baggage
checks, and new train connections. In other words, the Minnesota agents had ample opportunities here to advertise their
state and, at the same time, protect the new arrivals from
swindlers and "immigrant runners" who took every advantage
of the situation. The Board of Immigration eventually closed its
agencies in New York and Quebec but continued its middle
western operations for a number of years.

The Land-Grant Railroads

During the second half of the 1800s the sale of private land to
European immigrants became a special market for three
competitors—the major land companies, who bought up acreage on a speculative basis; the land-grant railroads, who sold
their government land titles to prospective farmers; and early
pioneers, who wanted to capitalize on rising land values and
push farther west.

The southern states were the special domain of the land
companies, which had acquired vast amounts of acreage and
launched a massive advertising campaign in search of new settlers. Their business operations soon faulted, however, when
disgruntled Swedes wrote home about the inadequate soil,
drought conditions, and the inhospitable climate. Meanwhile,
the land-grant railroads were opening up new territory in the
Middle West, and they came to have far greater significance for
Swedish immigrants.

How much acreage was involved in these sales transactions,
and what did this mean for homesteaders and land-grant settlers? Land-survey teams divided the territorial state map into a
chessboard pattern of townships measuring 6 miles to a side.
Each township consisted of 36 square-mile sections, each of
which amounted to an area of 640 acres. These sections were
numbered consecutively from 1 to 36, beginning at the northeast

corner of each township. Smaller acreage could be obtained by subdividing each section into units of 320, 160, 80, and 40 acres. According to the Homestead Act the maximum amount of acreage available to new settlers was a quarter section or 160 acres.

From the 1850s up to the early 1870s the federal government allocated vast quantities of land for railroad construction west of the Mississippi. These land grants varied in size from five to forty miles on both sides of the track, with railroad holdings limited to the odd-numbered sections in each land-grant area. The even-numbered sections were designated as homestead land, except for sections sixteen and thirty-six which were reserved for state financing of public education and school construction programs ("school land"). The railroads acquired ownership of their land sections with the laying of each new mile of track. Government land grants provided the economic backbone for these railroad lines. By selling their holdings the railroads not only found the means to pay for new construction but also established a demand for railroad travel all along the line. With these benefits in mind, the railroads took immediate steps to encourage new settlers to obtain government-owned homestead land. This was a comparatively easy task, especially in the land sections bordering on either side of the main line. Once these were settled, the railroads sharpened sales of their own land-grant holdings, which were now commanding higher prices.

Aside from the problems of financing new construction, the greatest concern of the railroad companies was a lack of manpower. In their eyes the ideal working man was the individual who labored long hours for modest pay and eventually settled down on land-grant territory. They soon discovered that Scandinavian immigrants matched this ideal in almost all respects. Free land, cheap land, and job opportunities were the major sales arguments of the land-grant railroads in their contacts with Swedish settlers, and it is no small coincidence that a Swedish-American heartland arose along the land-grant railroads west of the Mississippi and in the states of Michigan, Illinois, and Wisconsin.

Most of these railroads had drawn up detailed plans for advertising their territories and making them attractive to immigrant settlers. The largest enterprise was the Northern Pacific Railroad, which in 1864 received a land grant of some 47 million acres stretching along its lines of track between Lake Superior and the Pacific Ocean. Settlement was not only encouraged but simplified for the newcomer. Those who could afford it had their lands cleared ahead of their arrival, and there was even the option of buying ready-made fences and frame houses. The railroads also supplied free lodgings and offered discounts on rail travel to settlers and their families while land transactions were in progress.

In its settlement campaign of 1871 the Northern Pacific stressed the following incentives:

1. Maps and descriptions of land-grant holdings as well as homestead lands would be published in several languages.
2. All publications would be distributed free of charge in America and Europe by the company's own agents.
   The United States Department of State would also have a hand in publicizing the railroad and the steps it was taking on behalf of new immigrants.
3. Contacts would be made with steamship and railroad lines at home and abroad to ensure the distribution of settlement incentives and arrange for travel discounts to new settlers. The railroad would also work in close collaboration with the American and European press, professional and public men, as well as social and religious organizations on both sides of the Atlantic.

This was a highly ambitious, international sales campaign, to say the least, and part of the groundwork was laid by Swedish and Swedish-American agents and field representatives.

Hans Mattson, Land Agent

Between 1871 and 1873 Hans Mattson was employed as a land agent for the Lake Superior and Mississippi Railroad Company, which operated between St. Paul and Duluth, Minnesota. His activities provide a good example of the way in which European immigrants aided the cause of the American railroad interests. Mattson started work in the spring of 1871 and focused his attention on Isanti and northwestern Chisago Counties, where the railroad had 160,000 acres for sale. Swedes, the largest immigrant group in the area, had settled on government land before the railroad began to market its own land-grant sections. Mattson's first step was to send an agent to both counties to establish cordial relations and to gather information about the area from early settlers. At the same time the agent was to convince the early settlers of the interest they shared with the railroad in attracting new settlers and to outline the ways in which they could bring this about.

On the basis of his agent's report, Matsson launched an advertising campaign in the Swedish-American press, where he painted a glowing picture of the ten townships in western Chisago, eastern Isanti, and southern Pine and Kanabec Counties. Mattson called attention to the "forest land with good soil" and the "almost 200 Swedish families, most of them from Småland, Dalarna, and Norrland," who had started their own Swedish schools and churches. He also completed work on a special brochure, which was published in Swedish and Norwegian editions and was primarily intended for immigrant readers. Reference was made throughout the brochure to the achievements of Swedish pioneers and their ready knowledge of the area. The "Introduction," for example, pointed out that all information had been gathered from on-the-spot sources. Mattson went on to characterize the pioneers as living evidence of the fact that the area was suitable for habitation and that help was always at hand during the first difficult years on a frontier farm.

On Mattson's advice the Lake Superior and Mississippi Railroad hired a local agent, with offices in Rush City, to greet incoming settlers, aid them in the selection of their lands, and locate relatives and friends who were waiting for them. Above all, however, he was to stimulate a spirit of cooperation between old and new settlers. Mattson himself was very much aware of the lively correspondence between the Minnesota settlements and districts in Sweden and saw its importance in shaping the course of immigration. In a report to the railroad's board of directors on his forthcoming trip to Sweden Mattson stated: "I have already taken ample measures to guarantee extensive correspondence between settlers presently on your lands and their friends in Europe." Considering the high postal rates of the period it is not unlikely that postage expenditures were included under these "ample measures." During his stay in Sweden Mattson intended to make a first-hand inspection tour of the areas from which new emigrants could be expected, but he was also relying on the help of hand-picked Swedish settlers, who would be sent to Sweden and return later as the leaders of new immigrant parties. One of these assistants accompanied Mattson when he left for Europe in May, 1871.

In September of that year a pamphlet appeared in Kristianstad, Skåne, under the title, "Land for emigrants along the Lake Superior and Mississippi Railroad between St. Paul and Duluth in the State of Minnesota, North America." The author was "H. Mattson, Land Agent, Kristianstad." The American edition of this pamphlet had made constant reference to early Swedish settlements, and the same procedure was used in the Swedish version. Mattson mentioned that government land in the region "has been almost completely settled, primarily by Swedes." In other words, "the settler who buys railroad land does not have to carve out a home in the barren wilds but in the vicinity of a completed railroad line and in the midst of Swedish settlements." The Swedish pamphlet also described the pioneers as ideal neighbors who were willing to assist the new arrivals in every way possible. As in the American edition of his pamphlet, Mattson explained that the best land was located west of the railroad, from North Branch to a point north of Rush City, as well as in areas farther west and northwest. In the Swedish edition, however, he mentioned one additional location between Hinckley and Kettle River Stations in Pine County, with a center along the Kettle River. Here the land was cheaper because it was very sparsely populated.

Mattson's mention of this new area was in complete agreement with the plans he had presented to his employers before leaving Minnesota. Before the Chisago and Isanti townships were fully settled, immigration had to be routed to a new area along the line. According to Mattson's method, the first step was to establish small Swedish colonies which would then be used to attract other immigrants. By January, 1872, Mattson was ready to publish a revised edition of his Swedish pamphlet. A special chapter was devoted to the great forest fires that had ravaged the Midwest and played into the hands of Mattson's business competitors, who used them as a warning against settlement prospects in the Minnesota timberlands. In commenting on the fires, Mattson concluded that their consequences could only be positive ones: the railroad lands had been left untouched and would therefore attract the interest of the lumber industry. Even the great Chicago fire of 1871 was described as a fortunate turn of events, as it meant that Duluth would have a secure future ahead of it as "one of the largest and most important commercial centers of the West." While the new pamphlet also mentioned Hinckley as a suitable settlement area, it went on to promote the town of Thomson further north. Thomson's future lay in its water power from "one of the best waterfalls in the world," and Mattson gave this special emphasis.

Behind all of Mattson's activities on behalf of the Lake Superior Railroad lay the contributions of the early Swedish pioneers, which were constantly referred to as living proof of the possibilities for further settlement. That the Swedish population had gained almost sole control of the private economy in this area was a tribute to its strength in attracting other immigrants from the same regions in Sweden. The settlers themselves played an active role in all of this by corresponding with friends and relatives back home, or by promoting emigration in their capacity as visiting Yankees.

The arguments Mattson used in selling railroad land and promoting immigration did not dwell so much on the "end products," the quality of the soil, or the good wages offered by sawmills and early settlers. The most important argument was that Swedes had tested the product and found it to their liking. In his efforts to win settlers for the railroad, Mattson saw the necessity of building upon these Minnesota "converts" and encouraging them to move into new areas owned by the railroad, where they could act as magnets for further Swedish settlement.

There was another side to the picture, however, of which the railroad and the pioneers were both very much aware. Both parties hoped that the added population in the area would increase the value of their lands and boost the general economy. They were right. The railroad had no problem in selling its holdings in Isanti County, and the Swedes saw their property values rise as new farmers, farmhands, and neighbors flocked to the area.

Meanwhile the Northern Pacific Railroad was conducting its own settlement campaign in sections of northern Minnesota and North Dakota; the outcome made the company painfully aware of the role played by early pioneers in the process of immigration. The original intention was to attract Scandinavian settlers to the region, but as railroad construction was pushing into wilderness areas well beyond the reaches of any frontier settlements, the company could not generate any enthusiasm for the undertaking. In an effort to bridge the population gap, the railroad tried to implant homogeneous Swedish colonies. The project failed, however, partly because of the rumors of Indian uprisings that Duluth Swedes had been spreading among their countrymen. This had disastrous results for the company's sales operations and eventually led to its bankruptcy in the fall of 1873.

The ethnic composition of frontier settlements in Minnesota left its mark on Mattson's propaganda campaign in Sweden. Isanti County offers a colorful example of this, both in terms of geographic pull and religious affiliation. Most of its Swedish settlers came from Dalarna or Hälsingland, and its church life had a distinctly Baptist flavor. Both of these characteristics indicated the direction of Mattson's efforts in Sweden. Some of the Isanti colonists were persuaded to join Mattson's campaign in the capacity of visiting Yankees. Mattson himself worked closely with Karl Möllersvärd, the general agent for the Allan Steamship Line in Gothenburg and a former Baptist missionary to Dalarna and other parts of Sweden. At the close of this campaign, four new emigrant parties, the majority from Dalarna and Hälsingland, were ready to leave for Minnesota. According to the American census reports and the Lake Superior and Mississippi Railroad's land sales records, all of them settled near friends and relatives in Isanti County. The strong emigration of Baptists from the Orsa area in Dalarna illustrates the pull factor in no uncertain terms. Of the 102 Orsa residents who left Sweden under Mattson's leadership in May, 1873, as the last group of settlers to this land-grant region, nearly half were Baptists.

American Industry

The outbreak of the Civil War and the enlistment of industrial labor caused a severe manpower shortage in American industry. Industrialists hoped that the import of European contract labor would relieve the situation, but the experiment failed, largely because there were no guarantees that immigrant workers would respect the contract agreements and repay their employers' import costs. As a rule, industrialists could win very little by taking poor immigrants to court for breach of contract. Although this import legislation had been sanctioned by the American government, it was forbidden by law in Sweden. The Swedish government's position, however, was not the major reason why so few Swedish workers were contract laborers. As far as the workers were concerned, the labor clauses were highly unreasonable; they therefore drew the conclusion that they had every right to break their contracts. The experience of railroad workers in Minnesota provides one example. The Northern Pacific offered free transportation to its Minnesota camps in exchange for eight months' solid work without pay. When workers arrived in St. Paul they discovered they could cover their travel costs by working four months at regular Minnesota wages. As a result, they turned their backs on the railroad and refused to pay for anything. The fact that Swedish Americans came to their aid with information and moral support explains why breach of labor contracts was fairly common.

In Texas, however, the import of Swedish labor was crowned with some success. One of the most prominent and successful private enterprises was run by S. M. Swensson, who imported Swedes from Barkeryd in Småland and founded the Swedish settlement of Austin, Texas. Swensson's terms were free transportation in exchange for two years' labor. A more informal type of manpower recruitment won wide favor among Swedish Americans who forwarded prepaid tickets to friends and relatives back home. During the 1880s nearly half of all Swedish emigrants came to America on this basis. Whether all of the tickets listed in the emigrant agents' lists were repaid by emigrants after their arrival is an open question. Usually, however, prepaid tickets were a form of transport credit, in exchange for short-time work as farmhands or housemaids.

Even after the failure of contract labor legislation, American industry made little effort to recruit Swedish labor. Although steamship agencies advertised their job-hunting services, their information was usually unreliable or misleading. Some private interests, state governments, and various organizations opened their own labor exchanges in American ports and major inland cities, especially the "Swedish capital" of Chicago. The reputation of these firms and their promises of good wages, however, often left something to be desired. In the final analysis, Swedish Americans were the most important sources of information on the American labor market. Their assurances of job opportunities close to home or on their own farms were convincing enough for many emigrants.

The Atlantic Steamship Lines and the Emigrant Agents

Throughout the mass-emigration era, American and English steamship lines dominated the transport of Swedish emigrants over the North Sea and across the Atlantic. While immigration promoters used the immigration industry to expand their main-line activities, the Atlantic steamship companies considered it a matter of life or death. For this reason they did everything they could to promote emigration, and Sweden became a prime market target.

A total of ten different steamship companies were involved in the transport of Swedish emigrants. Some of them developed enormous operations. The giants during the 1880s were the

Cunard, Inman, Allan, and Guion Lines. Later competitors were the Anchor and American Lines as well as the Scandinavian-American Line, a Danish-Norwegian firm. In 1915 the Swedish-American Line opened the first direct service route between Sweden and America. All of these companies established agencies in ports of embarkation; at the most sixteen were active at any one time, although the average was usually ten. Because of its position in the emigrant traffic the western port city of Gothenburg became the headquarters for most of these agencies, but others were opened in Malmö and Stockholm. A special government permit, issued by the Swedish Board of Commerce, was required of each agent prior to the start of business operations.

An impressive network of subagents connected the main office with field operations throughout Sweden. Historians have recently uncovered the archives of the Larsson Brothers' Company in Gothenburg, which acted as agents for the Guion Line. Their records show that in 1882 the company had approximately 150 subagents. On the basis of this information, research has estimated that nearly fifteen hundred agency representatives were active in Sweden that same year. This means that at least one or two subagents were stationed in every single parish of southern and central Sweden. The district authorities had the power to issue permits to subagents, and as a rule applications were approved automatically.

The major responsibility of these subagents was to advertise the steamship lines' services, either by word of mouth or with the help of printed brochures and handouts. Their work was officially terminated when emigrants sent in their ticket deposits to the head agent. Subagents earned a commission of five to ten Swedish crowns (between $1.35 and $2.70) per emigrant. All financial transactions lay in the hands of the head agent, and once emigrants had arrived in Gothenburg, this agent drew up and signed the necessary emigration contract, which also served as a steamship ticket. According to Swedish law it was the agent and not the shipping lines who had legal custody of emigrant passengers and was responsible for their welfare. On the other hand, the companies usually helped their agents in paying the required security fee of up to 60,000 *riksdaler* ($1,500).

American interests soon discovered that this network of agents and subagents provided an excellent means of promoting their own services. Aside from distributing the shipping lines' colorful brochures, whose covers carried the picture of first-class ocean liners, subagents gradually acquired the role of salesmen for the glowing opportunities on the other side of the Atlantic—land, jobs, and the American way of life. The usual commission per emigrant was the only reward for their services. Head agents, on the other hand, received compensation from the companies they promoted, usually in the form of price reductions, which did not benefit their emigrant clients.

In choosing subagency personnel, agents were primarily interested in persons who stood in close contact with the Swedish public. Prime candidates were merchants, craftsmen, hotel- and innkeepers, as well as postal and railroad employees. Although the promotional possibilities were greater with these professions, it is unlikely that they had any real importance for the decision-making process behind emigration. This decision was usually far too crucial to be left to the stereotyped propaganda contained in shipping lines' brochures and paid advertisements. No matter how many subagents had been planted in a certain district, agents had no real way of forecasting the outcome of their efforts. In time, two groups of people, both of whom had their own interests at stake, assumed greater importance in stimulating emigration. Some Swedes accepted a standing offer from steamship line agents and earned free passage to America by recruiting the necessary party of ten to twenty emigrants. Others had already made the journey and established themselves as Swedish Americans, but accepted the offer of a round-trip ticket in exchange for their services as visiting Yankees.

One can easily imagine the ripple of astonishment and excitement in the Swedish countryside when former farmhands and prodigal sons came to town, talking and behaving in true Yankee fashion. They became the epitome of the American success story, representing the hope of every would-be emigrant. American business interests, quick to capitalize on these impressions, made a special point of hiring "successful" immigrants for such purposes. Hans Mattson is only one example: his return visit to Sweden in 1869, on behalf of one American railroad company, was directly responsible for the emigration of some four hundred fifty persons. Free-church leaders on both sides of the Atlantic also were regarded as suitable candidates for these propaganda missions.

In the long run, the local subagents became a superfluous link in this chain of travel information. The Swedish public grew so accustomed to the deluge of advertising brochures that they wrote directly to the main agents with all of their requests. In recent years Swedish historians have taken a closer look at the emigrant agents to evaluate their significance for the emigration process. Their studies reach the same conclusion: neither the agents nor their "product," transatlantic transport, had any independent impact on the extent of emigration. Both the agents and their subagents functioned more as travel consultants than as emigrant recruiters. It is true, of course, that mass emigration could not have developed without the services of the Atlantic steamship lines. Once this market had been created, however, companies were largely dependent upon the pull and push factors in both countries as a means of maintaining their sales. The momentum, in other words, was supplied by the supply of cheap land and job opportunities in America along with the sources of social unrest in Sweden. The same is true of the shipping lines' ticket-pricing policies. Public demand and emigrant volume alone determined what prices would be in effect, not the other way around. As a rule, prices increased during periods of peak emigration but decreased during periods of low emigration.

Swedish-American Interests in the Emigrant Traffic

Much has been said of the ways in which Swedish Americans came to the aid of American business interests in stimulating emigration. One can ask, however, just how conscious the immigrants were of their own role on this speculative market and whether they had any personal interests at stake. If they ever took matters into their own hands, what motives did they have?

On the surface, at least, their primary interests were both personal and emotional. The emigration of friends and relatives to this new continent answered a basic human need and reawakened feelings of togetherness, either as families or as whole villages. Equally important, however, were the more materialistic considerations. The arrival of new Swedish settlers to land-grant regions in Minnesota, for example, had a positive effect on land values, provided a backbone for population growth, and stimulated the general economy. The pioneers won new customers for farm produce, household wares, and industrial crafts, and they found a ready supply of cheap and reliable manpower. As one of the Minnesota pioneers confessed later on in life: "The first settlers made no bones about making profits on the new arrivals, selling them potatoes, beans, and hay at inflated prices."[3]

There are other examples of the ways in which Scandinavian settlers rallied to the cause of emigration promoters and land-development interests in their home states. In 1869, a new organization called "The Scandinavian Emigration Society of the State of Minnesota" came into existence. Its declared purpose was "to encourage immigration to this state and aid destitute countrymen" by coordinating the activities of local interest groups throughout Minnesota. The society took charge of the promotional appeals, while the local chapters supervised the relief program. Organizers and supporters launched a letter-writing campaign to friends and relatives back home, enclosing copies of Minnesota's Swedish newspapers. Later that same year the society distributed decorative letterhead stationery to the state's Swedish population. It also persuaded the state government to hire a Norwegian journalist who would tour the area and communicate his impressions to Scandinavian newspapers in the United States, Norway, and Sweden.

The importance of Swedish-American newspapers in this context is illustrated by the comments of one former emigrant in 1865: "Back home in Sweden there were only two people in my parish who received copies of the Chicago paper *Hemlandet.*

These were circulated throughout the district and were read from cover to cover, until they fell apart. For many years America reaped a rich harvest of emigrants from this same parish."[4] Newspapers such as *Hemlandet, Svenska Amerikanaren,* and *Minnesota Stats Tidning* were filled with encouraging articles and letters on American living conditions, all of which were guaranteed to win them a wide readership on the other side of the Atlantic.

Regardless of whether Swedish Americans championed their own interests or those of the immigration industry, their America letters and return visits were their most effective propaganda media.

It is difficult for us to imagine the situation a century or so ago, when letter-writing was considered a luxury for the rural population and the ability to write was not always a foregone conclusion. The arrival of any letter, especially from America, fed the curiosity of the entire community. It was read aloud for all to hear and even made the rounds of the parish district. At times a letter had to pass through many hands before its contents could be deciphered and understood. This was pointed out by a postmaster in Småland, who appealed to readers of the Chicago newspaper *Hemlandet* for a better approach to their correspondence: "The majority of emigrants cannot write Swedish, much less English. Notwithstanding this, certain emigrants, in order to advertise their proficiency in the new language to their relatives, put a good many English words in their letters; but as these words are incorrectly spelled and put together, the letters are unreadable to the recipient. He brings it to the preacher to have him read it. If he cannot, it remains unread."[5]

In most cases emigrants had no intention of spreading false rumors about America or their own living conditions. When they did write, their major concern was to pass on news of themselves to friends and relatives back home. This did not always guarantee, however, that readers could distinguish fact from fiction, and the high hopes that every emigrant had prior to departure were often fanned by glowing reports of material success. Even the simple statement that the new country matched one's initial expectations was accepted as proof that America had far more to offer than Sweden.

Although there were always two sides to the emigrant success story, some letter writers unconsciously omitted the darker side in an effort, perhaps, to justify their decision to emigrate. The fact that many of them were unaccustomed to expressing their thoughts on paper may also explain why their correspondence had more of an impact than they originally intended it to have. There were others, of course, whose only purpose was to stimulate a decision to emigrate; they did so by exaggerating the positive side of American life. This, then, was the major advantage of the America letters as compared to newspaper articles, advertising, and colorful brochures: the reader believed what he was told because it came from a friend or close relative.

The possibilities for exaggeration and outright distortion were even greater when Swedish Americans returned to their old home districts. Here they were greeted with a type of curiosity and excitement that almost elicited boasting and overacting. As far as the rural population could see, there was little reason to doubt the accuracy of their first impressions. The elegant clothes and cosmopolitan manners were every bit of an indication that a positive change had taken place and that America had to be the reason.

All of these factors—letters, newspaper articles, and return visits—meant that Swedish Americans were unexcelled as salesmen for America's open opportunities and as bearers of that inflammable disease known as "America fever."

6   Bound for America

The Atlantic Crossing

I advise you not to take a lot of linen cloth. Instead bring
plenty of tinware. Pack down some food so that you have
something to eat, in case you cannot stomach what they give
you at sea. Hardtack is good; also some cheese and dried meat.
Take along a food basket. When you arrive in America there
will be many who will approach you and offer you help. But
you must watch your step, for there are plenty of scoundrels
around who are ready to cheat the emigrants.

The advice of Maria Helene Jönsdotter to her sister, in a letter written
from Iowa in 1869.[1]

The first emigrants who traveled in groups usually sailed
directly to America from Sweden. Most of them left from
Gothenburg, although others chose Gävle, Söderhamn, or
Stockholm as ports of embarkation. Accommodations on board
these sailing vessels were primitive to say the least. Passengers
occupied the steerage section located directly above the cargo
hold with its load of iron bars. Although there was no set time
schedule, it usually took between one and a half to two months to
reach America.

During the 1850s and 1860s English and American shipping
lines acquired control of the emigrant traffic. By the 1860s
nearly all emigrants were sailing an indirect route by way of
England, and around the middle of the decade steamship travel

76

was common. The standard route for Swedish emigrants was by sea from Gothenburg to the English port city of Hull; by railroad from Hull to Liverpool; and, after several days' delay, by sea from Liverpool to the major immigrant harbors of New York, Boston, and Quebec.

Passenger comfort still left much to be desired at this time, and the Swedish press was particularly critical of conditions on board the English steamships. All passengers supplied their own food for the two-day journey across the North Sea to England. During the Atlantic crossing, however, all meals were provided free of charge. A typical weekly menu for steamship passengers in 1859 contained the following items:

> Sunday: a half pound of beef, porridge or pudding, dried fruit;
> Monday: pork, pea soup or boiled cabbage;
> Tuesday: beef, gruel or peas:
> Wednesday: beef, rice and molasses;
> Thursday: beef, porridge or pudding, dried fruit;
> Friday: beef, pork, pea soup or dried fruit;
> Saturday: herring or fish, peas or brown beans.

Each passenger was also allotted five pounds of white rusk biscuits per week and five and a half pounds of butter. Coffee was served in the morning and tea in the evening. Male passengers were entitled to one glass of *snaps* during the morning hours.

Though powered by steam the Atlantic liners of the 1860s and 1870s were equipped with sails that could be used for additional speed in brisk tail winds. As the century wore on and steam engines became more refined, sail cloth and canvas disappeared from the scene. By the late 1880s, only steamships were plying the transatlantic route, and in the process the voyage had been reduced to an average of ten to twelve days per crossing.

It may be hard for us to recapture the full panorama of impressions that greeted the Swedish landlubber during the Atlantic crossing. Some insights into the lives of midship passengers, however, are provided by a Swedish-English handbook called "The Emigrant's Interpreter" *(Utvandrarens Tolk)* which was published in 1881. An example of the advice provided by this handbook appears on the next page.

Swenska.	Engelska.	Uttal.
Ja, wi ha allt sådant, hwad wi behöfwa.	Yes, we are provided with all we want.	Jeß, oi ar prå wäjded oitth åhl oi oänt.
Kom med, så skall ni få.	Come along with me and you shall have.	Kömm älöng oitt mi, ännd ju schäll häwv.
Hwad få wi till frukost och afton?	What shall we hawe for breakfest and supper?	Hoött schäll oi häwv får bräkkfäst ännd söpper?
Te med skeppsbröd till.	Tea and biscuits.	Ti ännd biskits.
Detta köttet är dåligt, wi kunna ej äta det.	This meat is bad, we cannot eat it.	Thiß miht iß bädd, oi kännåt iht itt.
Det finnes ej något annat.	There are no other to have.	Thär ar nå ådher tu häwv.
Då måste wi klaga.	Then we must give in our complaint.	Thänn oi mößt givv inn aur kåmplänt.
Ja, gör det.	Well, do it.	Däll, du itt.
Alla passagerarne måste gå under däck och luckorna stängas; det blir storm.	All passengers must go down in the hold and the hatches be shut, there is an appearance of storm.	Åhl pässingers mößt gå daun in the hålld, ännd the hättschis bi schött, thär iß änn äppih=räns åvv stårm.
Jag kan ej gå ned; jag är så sjuk; jag kan ej stå.	I cannot go down; I feel very sick; I cannot stand on my legs.	Aj kännåt gå daun; aj sihl werri sick; aj kännåt stännd ånn mej läggs.
Aj hwad jag lider, jag tror jag dör.	Ah, what I suffer, I think I am dying.	Åh, hoått aj söfför, aj think aj äm däjing.
Ah, det går wäl öfwer.	Pshaw, it will pass.	Schåh, itt oill pahß.
Det war en ryslig storm.	This is a violent storm.	Thiß iß ä wäjälänt stårm.
Se tumlarne hoppa kring bogen på fartyget.	Look, the porpoises jump round the prow of the vessel.	Luck, the pårpåjses bjump raund the prå åvv the wässel.
Här förgås wi. Det är så qwaft. Få wi ej slippa ut?	Here we are lost. It is so sultry. Can we not get ont?	Hir oi ar låft. Itt iß så söltri. Känn oi nått gett aut?
Ej förr än stormen är öfwer.	Not before the storm has ceased.	Nått bifåhr the stårm häß sihsd.

Swenska.	Engelska.	Uttal.
Men innan deß äro wi qwäfda.	But in the meantime we are suffocated.	Bött in the mihn= täjm oi ar föffokäted.
Ah, har ingen fara.	Pooh, there is no danger.	Puh, thär iß nå dändjer.
Nu är stormen för= bi. Nu skall ni slippa ut.	New the storm is over. Now we shals let you out.	Nau the starm iß åv= ver. Nau oi schäll lett ju aut.
Hwad är det för ett land wi se der borta?	What land is its we see there?	Hoått länd iß itt oi si thär?
Det är Newfound= land. Wi äro snart framme.	It is Newfoundland. We are soon arrived.	Itt iß Njufaund= länd. Oi ar suhn arräjved.
Hwilken herrlig ut= sigt!	What a beautiful prospect!	Hoått å bjutifull pråspäkt!
Alla paßagerarne skola sprätta upp madraßerna och kasta halmen i sjön.	All passengers must rip up their mat- tresses and throw the halm into the sea.	Ahl päßingers mößt ripp öpp thör mät= träßes ännd thrå the hahm intu the si.
Hwad är det för hwita båtar?	What white boats are those?	Hoått oäjt båts ar thåhs?
Det är lotsbåtar.	It is pilot-boats.	Itt iß pejlåt=båts.
Hwilka äro de som komma här?	What are those co- ming here?	Hoått ar thås kå= ming hir?
Det är tulltjenste= männen.	That are the cu- stom-officers.	Thätt ar the kös= stomåfficers.
Ingen får gå från bord förr än det tillsäges.	Nobody is permit- ted to leave the ship before ad- vertised.	Nåbåddi iß permit= ted tu lihv the schipp bifår ad= värtejsed.
Gif hit nycklarne till era kistor och kof= fertar.	Give up the keys to your chests and trunks.	Givv öpp the kihs tu jur tjäßts ännd trönks.
Nu får ni gå i land.	Now you may go on shore.	Nau ju mä gå ånn schår.
Hwad heter detta ställe?	What do you call this place?	Hoått du ju kåhl thiß plähs?
Det heter Castlegar= den.	It is called Castle- garden.	Itt iß kåhld Käßl= gärden.

The hatches closed off the passenger quarters in the steerage section from the upper deck area. Passenger quarters were usually very primitive, both in appearance and function. They might best be described as large, communal sleeping areas, which gave little or no chance of privacy. Conditions improved somewhat as time went by, and an arrangement of small berths or alcoves became a standard feature on most ships. Up until the 1890s, however, when mass Swedish emigration reached its culmination, passenger comfort remained far from satisfactory.

Swedish emigrants complained less about these hardships than they did about the difficulties in dealing with fellow passengers from other countries. They had particularly negative impressions of the Irish and often referred to them in letters published in the Swedish press as "rough and uncivilized creatures." Their opinions must have had an impact in some shipping circles, for by the early 1870s Swedish emigrant agents began to insert in their advertising brochures special notices that advised Swedes that they "would not be thrown together with the Irish." The strange menus on board ship were also a sore point of contention, and certain emigrant agents specified the fact that all food was prepared "according to Swedish tastes and customs."

Up until World War I the vast majority of Swedish emigrants booked passage on English and American ships that sailed to America by way of Hull and Liverpool. It was not until 1915 that the Swedish American Line opened a direct service route between Gothenburg and New York. From that point on the liners *Stockholm, Kungsholm,* and *Gripsholm* assumed major control of the Swedish emigrant traffic.

Upon arrival in New York, Swedish emigrants caught their first glimpse of America at the eastern edge of Manhattan Island, the site of an imposing architectural structure called Castle Garden. This served as the clearing station for new arrivals during the greater part of the 1800s, and it was here that emigrants passed through customs and immigration control before making contacts with railroad company agents. During the 1890s the American immigration authorities moved their headquarters to Ellis Island, at the entrance to New York harbor.

Through its portals streamed the new waves of southern and eastern European immigrants around the turn of the century.

The Journey West

A combination of canal boats, river steamers, and railroads carried the early immigrants from the East Coast to destinations farther west. A typical itinerary during the 1850s included the following connections: New York to Albany (river steamer); Albany to Buffalo (train); and Buffalo to Chicago (steamer across the Great Lakes). Swedes bound for northern Minnesota during the 1870s often took the train from New York to Oswego on Lake Ontario, where they boarded a Great Lakes steamer for Duluth. From the mid 1860s, however, the railroads dominated the westward travel offering direct connections between New York and Chicago by special emigrant trains. "The Emigrant's Interpreter" came to the aid of Swedish passengers with a set of instructional phrases for railroad travel. One conversation read as follows:

> *At the railroad.*
>
> Where are the emigrant-cars?
> Here sir. Step in.
>
> Is this line much trafficed?
> Yes very much.
>
> Does it belong to a company?
> . . .
> May I offer you a cigarr?
> . . .
> Shall we not open the window?
> . . .
> Your railroads seen not to be built so solid
>   as that in Europe.
> This may be, but our cars are much more convenient;
>   you may walk about as you like, through th whole
>   train during the passage, and you enjoy of all
>   conveniences as on a steamer.
> Yes, that is true.
> . . .

At the station.

Passengers for the West change cars.

What shall we do?
Get out all of you!
We stop here till Monday.

It is easy to imagine how the average Swedish emigrant must have felt when confronted with this type of elevating conversation. The surprise was probably all his own if he never attempted to learn it by heart. He had time to practice, however, as the trip to Chicago from New York at that time took four to five days, with no less than three stops every day for meals. For most Swedes Chicago was the great transit station on the road west, but those who settled there soon transformed it into the world's third largest Swedish city.

Land agencies, railroad companies, and state interest groups were not the only ones who looked for new customers among immigrant arrivals. Some reception committees included members of the established immigrant community, who represented Chicago's boarding houses, express offices, and currency exchanges. They descended on their unsuspecting countrymen with a display of feigned understanding or paternalistic authority and literally convinced them to surrender their baggage receipts, climb aboard hired carriages, and spend the night at a boarding house. It made no difference whether the new arrivals had ever planned to stay in Chicago or were anxious to meet other train connections. Far less fortunate were the immigrants who arrived in Chicago with absolutely no idea of where they were headed. They fell the frequent victims of fly-by-night operators and their disreputable business practices. These circumstances made it all the more important that railroad representatives and travelers' aids were on hand to meet every emigrant train.

Many Swedes were forced to stay in Chicago for the simple reason that their money had run out. The May and June issues of Chicago's Swedish newspapers carried such familiar headlines as "The destitute have already arrived," "Our countrymen are starving." An article from 1868 described the situation in more detail:

> Between June 29 and July 6 a total of 1,570 Scandinavians arrived in Chicago. Departures during this same period were approximately 800. At present 16 destitute families have found places to stay at the Michigan Central Railroad warehouse. They are waiting to hear from relatives in Minnesota and Wisconsin who have promised to send them money. Several weeks have gone by now, and they are no longer able to provide for themselves. One day last week they received food donations worth thirteen dollars. This week, however, 5 children in these families have died of cholera.[2]

However disturbing such scenes may have been, the Chicago Swedes showed great concern for their needy countrymen. At the end of the 1860s two Scandinavian relief associations were founded to handle such crises.

Whether or not they experienced the hardships of being stranded in a large and unfamiliar city, most Swedish immigrants eventually pushed on from Chicago for points farther west, primarily the older Swedish settlements and the rising industrial cities of the Upper Northwest. Along the way some of them received help from Swedish benevolent societies and relief committees, while others found relatives and friends to take care of them for the time being. There were always those, however, who would not be satisfied until they had established themselves on the frontier, and after a while they moved on to homestead areas, railroad teams, and lumberjack camps.

Perhaps the best way of illustrating the stages in this emigration process, beginning with the Atlantic crossing and ending with the arrival in the Middle West, is to reproduce the story of one emigrant's odyssey, as told in her own words. The following letter was written in 1869 by twenty-one year old Sara Mathilda Samuelson, who emigrated that year to America from Östergötland. She was accompanied by her maternal aunt and two cousins who settled on a farm in the state of New York. Sara Mathilda journeyed on her own to Galesburg, Illinois, where other relatives were living.

Galesburg, June 13, 1869

Dearly beloved parents and my dear brothers and sisters,

May you always be well, that is my daily wish for you all. I must thank you all for the last time I was at home with you all. You can't imagine how much I have seen since I parted with my mother at Linköping the 10th of May. Then I started my long trip to America, but on the 10th of June I ended my trip, so my trip to America lasted a whole month. You asked me to write about how things were on my trip, but it isn't easy for me to write about everything.

I came to Göteborg on the 13th, then I left there the 14th when I went across the North Sea and arrived in Hull on the 17th. I went from Hull the 18th when I traveled by railroad across England to Liverpool where I arrived the same date. I had to stay over in Liverpool from the 18th to the 21st—so that was three days.

On the 21st, which was a Friday, I went on the great ocean and crossed it in 12 days. Thus, I arrived in New York on June 3rd. But now I shall let you know that I had good health during the trip, for which I must thank my gracious God, and for the good fortune I had, for I haven't lost a penny's worth of anything on my whole trip.

People were certainly sick on the North Sea and they vomited all over. So wherever one went it was the same. You may be sure it wasn't always pleasant. I was on two ships; on the first I had to provide my own food (which you knew already at home), but when I got on the second ship, food was provided for us. But you may be sure that it wasn't easy for me to consume the kind of food they had, so I would rather eat from my own food bag as long as it lasted. But it was soon gone and the same for my aunt. Thus when I came to New York I had to use my money [for food] from New York to Galesburg. All my money is gone now, but I am in Galesburg.

I went from New York on June 4th in the evening and we came to Chicago the 9th—that was four days. There we had to be from the morning until 12 o'clock at night before we could go on to Galesburg. I arrived in Galesburg at 8 o'clock in the morning of Thursday, June 10th. Then I entered [the home of] Sara and Carl Gustaf in Galesburg, so you can now be sure that I am in America all right, and that I have good health and feel well up to this moment of writing. Now I must tell you what my first task was: it was to sit down and eat! On the second day I washed my clothes and on the third day I was at Nils Asp's and scrubbed [the word "skude" in the original may be intended for "skurde"-skurade]. So it isn't difficult for me. Now I must let you know that I can stay at the home of my cousin Nils Asp for a month until I can get some employment. This is a good thing for me, you may be sure, so that I can learn the language, for it can't be learned quickly, I assure you. I had enough dollars left from my trip so that I bought myself a dress as it is called in English [she wrote *därs*, in an attempt to reproduce the English *dress*], but now all my money is gone.

Now I will close my writing for this time, with a dear greeting from me to all of you. Greet all my acquaintances and tell them I am well. Write at the first [opportunity].

Gusta's Sara sends greetings to Falvik, and I can greet you from all three of the Asp boys.

When you write let me know how you have it in Sweden. Aunt Anna is in New York; they get 10 dollars a month all three.[3]

"There at last!"

Once they had chosen a place to settle, immigrant farmers and their families spent the first months clearing the land and felling timber for their first rude cabins. When winter approached, the head of the family was usually forced to find work with the railroads or lumber companies, leaving his wife and children to manage on their own for months on end. Though conditioned by necessity, this separation was particularly hard on immigrant women, who had little or no knowledge of English and were accustomed to the simple but secure surroundings of the Swedish countryside. Other families, who arrived in this country with sufficient savings, spared themselves many of these hardships by buying land in more populated areas.

It was not unusual for three or four families to join forces on the American frontier by establishing a closely knit farm community. For the first few years all work was performed on a collective basis, each family helping the others in purchasing farm equipment, building log cabins, and breaking the land. When money ran short after the harvest season, one family head would stay in the area while the others looked elsewhere for work. Their earnings supplied food for the winter months and seed for the new planting season. This collective arrangement was only temporary, lasting three or four years, by which time each family had become self-sufficient.

Deciding where to settle was an important step for Swedish farm families, and many of them sent one or two relatives ahead to scout out the possibilities and make arrangements for the rest to follow. In most cases the responsibility fell to the husband or eldest son, who went to work for the railroads or lumber companies to earn ticket money for the immediate family. In some cases, however, daughters had an equally important role to play. One example of this comes from a letter written in 1869 by Hans Mattson to his wife in Red Wing, Minnesota. Describing his visit to a close relative in Skåne Mattson wrote:

> They are a very large family, and almost all of them want to join us in Minnesota. Pehr Pehrsson also wants to come, and he is sending his two youngest daughters with me this spring to scout the possibilities. They are terribly nice girls and would like to find positions with good American families. I am therefore asking you, Chersti, and sister Anna, to keep them in mind when you hear of such positions. I have promised them that they will have no difficulties in finding homes and friends in our midst. It is likely that the rest of the family will come to Lake Ripley at some later date.[4]

Most emigrants from rural Sweden were accustomed to hard work, but the unfamiliar surroundings and the language difficulties often created hardships for them during their first years in America. The experiences of one Swedish immigrant in 1869 were probably shared by many others.

> I went to work for the railroad with a promise of $2 per day. It wasn't until that moment that I realized who I really was—an immigrant, and nothing better than a "greenhorn." To begin with, the weather was so unbearably warm that few of us newcomers could stand the work. Our camps were located in

the woods, and there we were fed and lodged for $4 a week which was deducted from our pay. But the food was so bad that none of us could live on it. When pay day came and we figured we had some $20 to our credit, in addition to food, all we were left with was $7. There was nobody around who could speak a word of English, and so it was impossible to change things.[5]

Another immigrant characterized his life us a lumberjack and railroad worker in these terms: "We've all read about and admired the exploits of King Karl XII and his men, but I can tell you that I've stamped about in the same frost-biting cold and weathered the same hardships glorified in the history books."

As time wore on, more and more Swedish immigrants settled in American cities, where they usually found relatives and friends who could help them adjust to their new surroundings. Those skilled in a special trade or profession often had difficulties in finding the same kind of work in America. "My countrymen taught me never to admit that I didn't know how a certain job was to be done."[6] That was the comment of one Swede who immigrated during the 1890s. Others like him probably followed the same rule-of-thumb. It came almost as a shock to most emigrants that their first wages were well below the average for American workers. This was usually a result of language difficulties and misunderstandings connected with labor contracts. Under these circumstances one can easily understand why many immigrants became homesick. This feeling, however, rarely found its way into letters back home but, instead, was shared with friends in America or committed to memory. One example of this is found in the diary of a Halland emigrant, who summarized his first six months in America with the following tersely worded sentences:

> I began work and earned a little money in Colchester, Connecticut, on June 14, 1888. I was 26 years old. It was hard work, it was terribly hot, and I was incredibly homesick for Sweden.
>
> Things have gotten a little better now, as I write. Colchester, January 3, 1889,
> Emil A. Johansson.[7]

7   Who Were They and
       Where Did They Settle?

Geographic Distribution in the United States

As used by the United States Bureau of Statistics, the term "Swedish Americans" designates persons who were born in Sweden and later came to America (first-generation immigrants) or persons who were born in this country to Swedish or part-Swedish parents (second-generation immigrants). The statistical tables include both of these groups but eliminate the third generation due to problems with the American census statistics. Special attention has been focused on the statistics for 1890, 1910, 1930, and 1970. (See Figure 5.) The 1890 statistics show the settlement distribution of the first great waves of Swedish emigrants, most of whom came from rural areas. The 1910 statistics reflect the impact of emigration by Swedish industrial labor between 1890 and 1910. By 1930 mass emigration had come to a halt, and almost all of those who came during the peak years of the 1860s and 1880s had disappeared from the picture. Included in the 1930 statistics is the continued emigration from Swedish industry during the early 1920s. Statistics for 1970 illustrate the geographical distribution of Swedish Americans in an era when jet travel and international charter flights bring many of them to Sweden. Third-generation immigrants are excluded from these statistics.

Around 1890 the north central region with its Homestead Triangle, land-grant railroads, and Swedish pioneer settlements

88

became the geographical center of the Swedish-American population. By this time Minnesota had surpassed the mark set by Illinois in the 1880 census as the state with the largest Swedish immigrant population. In terms of relative statistics, however, Minnesota acquired its unchallenged ranking as early as 1870 and has held that position ever since. The 1890 census showed that 12.6 percent of Minnesota's population were Swedish Americans, and despite the fact that they were outnumbered by the Germans, who commanded a 25.5 percent share of the population that same year, Swedes began to call Minnesota the "Swedish state." Considered as a whole, Scandinavians were the largest ethnic group in Minnesota, having surpassed the Germans as early as 1870. By 1910, 45 percent of the Swedish-American population had settled in the north-central region, but their numbers had increased at a much more rapid rate in other parts of the United States. This was especially true of the

Figure 5. The Regional Distribution of the Swedish-American Population.

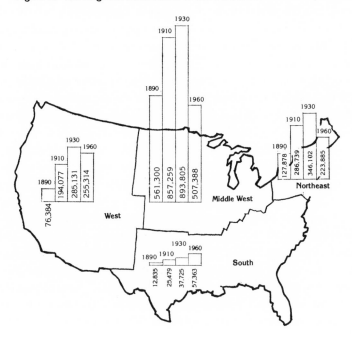

Rocky Mountain states, which were settled by Swedish pioneers, but it also applied to the timber regions of the Northwest and the fruit orchard districts in California. At the same time, immigrants from Swedish industry were streaming to the northeastern states, where New York and Massachusetts ranked high in the statistical columns. The overall population growth in these states, however, nullified the proportional effect of this immigration.

The settlement trends established by 1910 have continued through the 1930s up to 1970. The traditional concentration of Swedish Americans in the north central region and the Rocky Mountain states has thinned out, as more and more have moved to the industrial states along the Atlantic seaboard and the resort areas of the Pacific Coast and the Deep South. The explosive post-war growth of such states as California and Florida highlights a special dimension of this population movement. Scores of retired Swedish Americans have filtered into the South and West, lured by the hospitable climate and inexpensive life style.

Even during this century Minnesota has occupied a special position as the state with the largest percentage of Swedish Americans. Its closest competitors are the states of Washington, the Dakotas, Nebraska, and Illinois. In terms of absolute figures, Illinois is the only state that has come close to challenging Minnesota's position. The 1970 statistics show, quite naturally, that first- and second-generation Swedish immigrants represent a rapidly declining share of the population in most states. Almost forty-five years have passed since the last of these generations crossed the Atlantic, and most of them are well past the age of retirement. In 1950, for example, first-generation Swedish immigrants averaged between sixty-three and sixty-four years of age.

Were one to characterize Swedish Americans as a predominantly rural or urban population, one's initial impulse would be to classify them as rural. This was, in fact, the case during the 1880s. Although Scandinavians have always been among the least urbanized immigrant groups, Swedish Americans have nevertheless shown the greatest frequency to settle in urban areas. As early as 1910 no less than 60 percent of all Swedish immigrants lived in cities, and this pattern has kept pace with the overall process of urbanization in American society. In 1950, Norwegians had the lowest percentage of urban residents among all the major immigrant nationalities. Swedes ranked second to last on the list. In both cases, however, the majority lived in cities—67.4 percent of the Norwegians and 74.9 percent of the Swedes. For all immigrant groups in 1950, the average number of urban residents was 83.7 percent

Compared with the first arrivals, second-generation immigrants were less inclined to settle in urban areas, with Norwegians represented by 57.7 percent and Swedes by 68.8 percent. This is probably because first-generation immigrants moved to the cities when they reached retirement age, while their children stayed on to manage the family farm.

It is commonly held that Swedes preferred to settle in areas that were an exact copy of the Swedish countryside they knew so well. Swedish author Fredrika Bremer gave substance to this belief as far back as 1850, when she designated Minnesota as "the New Scandinavia," and for the very same reasons. If she were right, the Plains States west of the Mississippi, large sections of Illinois, and the "Swedish" states to the east would have almost nothing in the way of a Swedish population. Minnesota's scenic surroundings had hardly any significance for its enormous attraction of Swedish settlers, even though Swedes may have found it easier to adjust to conditions here than elsewhere. The decisive factor was the timing of mass Swedish emigration, which happened to coincide with the expansion of the American frontier and the opening of prime farm land in the state of Minnesota. The same is true of settlement patterns in other states.

Once the frontier had reached the Pacific, however, and the immigration of Swedish farmers began to decline, the economic geography of certain states acquired significance for immigrants' settlement preferences. There are striking similarities at times between the economic structure of emigrants' native districts and that of their new homes in America. One example can be cited from a recent research study of emigration from Örebro *län*. Rural emigrants tended to settle in the agricultural states of Iowa and Kansas, while those from industrial areas made their way to the manufacturing cities of Massachusetts and Pennsylvania. The same pattern is found among emigrants from Västernorrlands *län:* farmers and their sons emigrated to the prairies of the Midwest, while sawmill workers blazed a path to the timber industries of the northern United States and Canada. The expansion of American industry after 1900, however, increased the demand for manpower and caused greater numbers of rural Swedish emigrants to settle in industrial areas.

Other examples of this economic phenomenon can be found among those who settled in the industrial Northeast and reestablished themselves in their former trades and skills. In some cases a strong emigration tradition developed between particular Swedish districts and certain northeastern cities, of which Worcester, Massachusetts, is a good illustration. Large numbers of Swedes began immigrating to this city in 1880, and around 1900 they were ten thousand strong, representing one-tenth of the population. Two separate areas of Sweden became involved in this population movement at a very early stage, and each had ties to important Worcester industries. At the close of the 1860s a group of pottery makers from Höganäs in Skåne arrived at the Norton Pottery Works. Their example was followed by so many others from the same area that Swedes rapidly became the primary labor force in Worcester's pottery, and later abrasives, industry. Meanwhile, one of the owners of Worcester's largest iron works, the Washburn & Moen Company, paid a visit to Sweden's iron-producing regions and encouraged workers to emigrate to Worcester. The result was a steady stream of immigrants from the iron industries of central Sweden, particularly Örebro and Värmlands *län.*

Chicago, on the other hand, with its widely differentiated economic profile, did not attract immigration from any special region in Sweden. Although Swedes rapidly assumed control over two of the city's occupational branches, domestic help and the construction trades, neither of these developments was related to immigration from specific Swedish districts.

The westward push of the American frontier and the timing of European arrivals to this country were of decisive importance for the spread and concentration of immigrant settlements. The effects can still be seen in the geography of states stretching from the Middle West to the Pacific. Small pockets of early Swedish immigrants, for example, developed in the eastern and southern portions of certain states. From here the settlement pattern spread westward, keeping pace with the arrival of other immigrant groups. The fact that so many of these early settlements still exist is due to the "stock effect," or their magnetic attraction of new immigrants over the course of time. Despite a continual loss of population, usually to states farther west, they managed to retain a distinctly ethnic flavor throughout the mass emigration era. The emigration tradition established by the earliest arrivals guaranteed a flow of new settlers from the same Swedish districts and explains why Isanti County, north of St. Paul, became known as the "American Dalarna" and why neighboring Chisago County gained the reputation as the "American Småland."

Similar patterns can be seen in Wisconsin, where settlement spread westward from the southeast, towards the Mississippi River, and then farther north. The Germans were the first to arrive, and their settlements continue to dominate the southern and eastern sectors of the state. They were followed by the Norwegians, Wisconsin's second largest ethnic group, with major concentrations in the south and southwest. Then came the Swedes, who settled in the west and northwest, and finally the Finns, whose settlements can still be found in the northernmost parts of the state.

This formation of relatively homogeneous ethnic colonies or enclaves also characterized settlement patterns in urban areas, and the way in which these enclaves moved about the city over the course of time reveals a great deal about immigrant adjustment to American society. A prime example is to be found in the city of Chicago, which in 1900 was considered the home of one out of every ten Swedish Americans and, next to Stockholm itself, the world's largest Swedish city. According to Ulf Beijbom's study of the Chicago Swedes, the life of the Swedish enclave can be divided into three periods. The first was marked by the primitive settlements of the 1840s and 1850s, when the Chicago pioneers lived as destitute squatters in the immigrant slum along the north shore of the Chicago River. During the

1860s the enclave moved farther north, centering around Chicago Avenue, which soon became "Swedish Farmers' Street" for the surrounding "Swede Town." This location proved to have a far brighter future than the squatter existence of the earlier period. Swedes bought their own homes and found steady, though low-paid, jobs within easy walking distance.

The third and last period in the enclave's history came at the end of the 1800s, when Swede Town began to deteriorate to a slum housing area and residents felt the pressure of newly-arrived immigrants from southern and eastern Europe. The more affluent members of the community moved on to such suburbs as Lake View, Englewood, and Hyde Park, where they were joined by some of the new arrivals who were somewhat better situated than the Chicago pioneers and could therefore avoid the slum districts around Swede Town.

Social Origins and the Adjustment to New Surroundings

Can it be said that all Swedish emigrants shared some things in common, and if so, just what were these characteristics? No one has ever made an exhaustive study of the matter, but certain generalizations can be made in an effort to shed more light on the emigrants as persons.

Most emigrants were of fairly sound physical health, and in that respect they probably ranked well above the average for the Swedish population during the 1800s. One would also have to assume that they had both the stamina and the will power to adjust to their new surroundings. It is a fact that younger people find it easier to adapt to new situations and the demands of hard work. A look at the age spread among Swedish emigrants shows that most of them were from twenty to twenty-four years in age. The second and third largest groups were from twenty-five to twenty-nine and from fifteen to nineteen.

Research into the marital status of the average emigrant discloses a number of interesting facts. No less than two-thirds of those involved in the group emigrations of the 1840s and 1850s were married couples and their children. This was perfectly normal, as frontier life demanded the resources of all family members. As time wore on and more and more emigrants came from nonagricultural occupations, the number of family emigrants decreased. In fact, families became something of an undesirable burden during an emigrant's first years in America. Around 1900 more than two-thirds of all emigrants were unmarried, with the greatest increase coming from single women. The reason for this was the demand for maids in American households which, in turn, had an effect on the sex ratio of emigrants in large urban areas. The situation among Chicago Swedes in 1880 offers a prime example: in that year there were 136 women per 100 men aged 15 to 19 and 117 women per 100 men aged 20 to 29.

During the 1840s and 1850s most rural emigrants belonged to two distinct social classes, either landowning farmers or tenant farmers. Throughout the rest of the century, however, the largest percentage of rural emigrants came from the lower, landless classes. Although the Swedish emigration statistics do not provide a reliable picture of the occupational breakdown among rural emigrants, there is every indication that approximately 80 percent belonged to an agricultural proletariat that had no prospects of gaining access to farm land either through inheritance or by rental agreement. Included in this group were farm hands, maid servants, lodgers, day laborers, and the sons and sons-in-law of landowning farmers.

Despite these conditions, emigration did not always loom as the most obvious solution for the agricultural proletariat. There was still the alternative of moving to the cities. While the journey to America was the longer of the two alternatives, one can always speculate whether it placed more demands on a person than migration within Sweden. Wasn't America more of a household word than Stockholm? Did not the average Swede have far more friends on the other side of the Atlantic than he did in his own capital city? Who was the more daring of the two—the farm hand who migrated to a large or medium-sized Swedish city and entered the ranks of industrial labor, or the farm hand who made a complete break with familiar surroundings, emigrated to America, and established himself on his own farm? All of these questions are well worth the asking but cannot be answered here.

Considering the background of Swedish emigration and the types of people who became emigrants, it is not surprising that farming was the major livelihood of Swedish Americans during the 1800s. In fact, the United States census statistics for 1900 show that of all American immigrant groups, only the Danes and Norwegians surpassed the Swedes in this occupational sector. Although we lack complete, detailed statistics on all occupational sectors around the turn of the century, available reports indicate that approximately 40 percent of the Swedish-American population (first and second generations) was engaged in farming as opposed to 32 percent in industry. If we separate these two generations we find, not surprisingly, that most first-generation immigrants owned their own farms, while most of the second generation settled for work as farm hands or drifted to industry. In 1900, Swedish Americans were employed in three major industrial branches—iron, building construction, and lumber. The last branch in particular employed large numbers of Swedish carpenters and sawmill workers. Compared with other immigrant nationalities, Swedes also had a surprisingly high regard for the tailoring profession. Around 1900 no less than 57 percent of all employed Swedish-American women were domestics. A dramatically smaller percentage held employment as seamstresses and dressmakers, while the third largest group (16 percent) was engaged as laundry workers.

Since the beginning of this century the urbanization process has reduced the ranks of the Swedish-American farming population. By 1950 only thirteen thousand of the approximately one hundred twenty thousand first-generation Swedes were still engaged in farming, and of those, ten thousand five hundred owned their own farms. Meanwhile, domestic service remained the primary occupation of Swedish-American women. That same year the majority (45,540) of the Swedish-American labor force could be classified under the headings of foremen and craftsmen, while over eleven thousand managed their own businesses. Industrial labor employed nearly twenty-eight thousand Swedes, and public-service jobs approximately eight thousand.

Postwar Swedish immigrants are radically different from their predecessors, both in terms of their social origins and the nature of their stay in this country. They are generally well educated and well informed about American living conditions, due largely to the impact of the mass media. Their ready knowledge of English simplifies the adjustment to American society, and they have little need to associate with other Swedes outside their places of work. The term "temporary emigrants" is perhaps the best way of describing their intentions in the United States: The opening of world markets for Swedish corporations, for example, has led to the transfer of business executives to American subsidiaries. To work in the United States they are required to have immigrant visas, and the same is true of university researchers, doctors, engineers, and other professional people, most of whom stay only long enough to explore the possibilities of a career or permanent residence in America. The prospects of study, travel, and part-time work have also attracted large numbers of Swedish teenagers and given them the opportunity to satisfy a natural curiosity about the country that makes newspaper headlines around the world. Whatever their reasons for immigrating, most of these newcomers are drawn to such metropolitan centers as New York, Washington, Chicago, Seattle, San Francisco, and Los Angeles as well as the resort areas along the southern California coast.

Swedish Place-Names in the United States

Problems of identification make it almost impossible to estimate the number of Swedish place-names in the United States. Names such as *Johnson City, Mount Andersson, Peterson Creek,* or *Swanson* could just as well be Danish, Norwegian, or Anglo-American as they could be Swedish. All too often the lack of written documentation obscures the history of place-names which are unmistakably Swedish.

The tradition of assigning place-names in America is not only more recent than but also very different from the practice in Europe. In terms of geographical concentration, for example,

America has an average of one place-name per square mile, while Sweden has approximately one hundred fifty for the same area. At the same time, large stretches of the American continent—mountains, deserts, and glaciers—have yet to be named on the map. In some cases older place-names are being changed by state and local officials to avoid confusion. Mud Lake, for example, was originally the collective name for a chain of lakes in the state of Michigan. In 1942 a local official decided to rename one of them as Gyttja Lake, because "*gyttja* is the Swedish word for mud."

A Swedish researcher by the name of Otto R. Landelius is responsible for the most comprehensive study of Swedish place-names in the United States.[1] According to his research there are more than eight hundred such place-names on the American map, most of them concentrated in areas settled by early Swedish pioneers. The rest have no connection with Swedish immigration and, as a rule, are the invention of non-Swedes. Dannemora, for example, a mining town in eastern New York State, traces its name to an American mine owner in 1850 who happened to be interested in Swedish mining operations. The name has rich traditions, for the original Dannemora, located in northern Uppland province, has been an iron-ore producing region for some five hundred years. The town of Kalmia, nestled along the slopes of the Appalachians in North Carolina, was named as late as 1932. It was previously called Lotta in memory of the postmaster's daughter-in-law. The word *kalmia* stems from a plant of the same name that thrives in that area and traces its own ancestry to the Swedish traveler Pehr Kalm, who once studied under the famous botanist Carl von Linné. Swedish singer Jenny Lind's acclaimed concert tour of America in 1851 inspired several place-names, including the town of Jenny Lind, located in the very un-Swedish state of Arkansas. Other place-names that fit this description are Olson Creek and Olson Mountain in Montana, both named after Swedish-born Charley Olson, who worked as a cook for the surveying teams in that state around the turn of the century. Mount Nystrom in Wyoming, a 12,356-foot peak, almost twice the altitude of Sweden's highest point, was named in 1877 by

F. M. Endlich of the Hayden survey to honor the family of his fiancée.

Over two hundred Swedish place-names, representing one-forth of Landelius' research, are found in Minnesota. Readers of Vilhelm Moberg's emigrant novels will recall Chisago County, north of St. Paul, perhaps the most Swedish colony in the United States and one dotted with the names of Swedish pioneers. The town of Lindstrom, for example, was named after Hälsingland emigrant Daniel Lindström; Almalund, after Småland emigrant John Almquist; and Stark, after a Västergötland emigrant, Lars Johan Stark. Wallmark Lake and Ogren Lake are only two of many lakes in Chisago County which were named after Swedish pioneers. A large number of Swedish cities also have counterparts on the Minnesota map, including Borgholm, Kalmar, Malmo, Ronneby, Upsala, Falun, and Stockholm.

Kittson County, located in the far northwest corner of Minnesota, attracted a large number of Skåne emigrants, who settled in three adjacent townships called Tegner, Svea and Skane. Jockmock Lake, to the northeast, traces its origins to the Swedish hermit, Gust Hagberg, nicknamed "Jockmock," who was still living in the area around the turn of the century. An example of place-names derived from infant christenings is Alma township in Marshall County, named after Alma Dahlgren, the daughter of a Swedish pioneer and the first child born in the area. In 1897 the Swedish North Pole explorer, S. A. Andrée, made world newspaper headlines with his daring but ill-fated balloon expedition across the Arctic Sea. A year later a small Minnesota community opened its first post office under the name of Andree.

The northwestern sections of Wisconsin are equally rich in Swedish place-names. Stockholm township, one of the Midwest's earliest Swedish settlements, was founded by the somewhat legendary Karlskoga emigrant, Erik Pettersson, also known as "King Erik" and "the King of Stockholm." Pettersson may well have had challengers to his royal title, as there are other Stock-holms scattered throughout the United States.

One example of the smaller flora of Swedish place-names in

the state of Iowa is the town of Munterville, named in 1870 after Magnus Munter, a Småland emigrant, Iowa pioneer, school teacher and lay preacher. New Sweden, in Jefferson County, represents not only a very common type of Swedish place-name but also an immigrant watchword or social program, the creation of a new and better Sweden on the American continent. It is, in fact, none other than the Peter Cassel colony which lives on in this place-name and gives it the distinction of being the oldest surviving example of nineteenth-century Swedish settlements on the American map.

Washington state has the largest interlocking series of Swedish settlements west of the Rocky Mountains and boasts approximately fifty Swedish place-names. The towns of Edwall and Forsell are both named after Swedish pioneers, while Hoogdal traces its origins to three Swedish emigrants from the Ytterhogdal area of Hälsingland. Mabana, a small community in northwestern Washington, would appear to be a typically American construction were it not for the fact that its inspiration came from Mabel Anderson, the daughter of a Swedish pioneer. Parts of her first and last names form the basic syllables, with an extra *a* added at the end.

The flora of Swedish place-names in the United States is both a picturesque and warmly personal document over the lives of Swedish-American pioneers and the achievements of distinguished men and women in Swedish history. Their memory will be kept alive on the American map long after the Swedish language has died out in American society.

8   Swedes Become Americans

Swedes in Politics

Before 1850 most Swedish Americans, like the majority of other immigrant nationalities, were strong supporters of the Democratic party, as the Democrats happened to be the most outspoken champions of immigrant interests in this country. The birth of the Republican party in the mid-1850s, however, changed this situation rather dramatically. Scores of Swedish voters were attracted by the Republicans' antislavery platform and their promise of free land to new settlers. The Swedish-American press, which came into being about the same time, rallied to the Republican cause by championing the slogan of "a nation of free men, free homes, and free work." The swing to Republican principles included a deep-rooted allegiance to the leadership of Abraham Lincoln, which almost became a type of religious hero worship after his death.

The Republicans dominated the American political scene during the rest of the 1800s and past the turn of the century, but were slow in repaying the Swedes for their solid support. Up to 1900, in fact, only a small handful of Swedish Americans ever held any major political office in the party. There were several reasons for this. The party leadership seemed to feel that there was little need to attract Swedish voters by way of extra favors or the promise of political office. Then, too, comparatively few Swedes had arrived in the United States before the Civil War, and a distinguished military record was almost a necessity for any political candidate during the decades after 1865. Typically enough, the first Swede to make a career in state politics was also one of the few Swedish colonels in the Union Army, namely Hans Mattson, elected Minnesota's secretary of state in 1869.

The first Swede to make a breakthrough in national politics was Republican John Lind of Minnesota, elected to a first term in the House of Representatives in 1886 and reelected twice. In the 1890s Lind changed parties to become the opposition's candidate for governor of Minnesota in the 1896 election. His defeat did not stop him from running again in 1898, and when the ballots were counted Lind had become the state's first Democratic governor since 1860.

Lind's personal break with the Republican party had repercussions for a long-standing tradition among Swedish-American voters and set the stage for other political careers. Democrat John Albert Johnson is perhaps best remembered in Swedish-American circles after 1900. Twice elected governor of Minnesota, he was generally considered a candidate for the Democratic presidential nomination in 1912. His untimely death in 1909, however, thwarted the hopes of the Swedish-American electorate, and the nomination went to Woodrow Wilson, who won the presidency from a divided Republican party.

Another distinguished Swedish-American politician was Charles A. Lindbergh, father of the Atlantic flyer and a five-term member of the House of Representatives. Raised in Minnesota, Lindbergh had immigrated to America as a small child in 1860 together with his father, Ola Månsson, a controversial member of the Swedish Farmers' party from Gärdslösa in Skåne. Lindbergh was elected on the Republican ticket in 1906 to the United States House of Representatives and served there for five terms until March, 1917. A rugged individualist on matters of political principle, he often clashed with the Republican leadership. His opposition to the American entrance into World War I provides a prime example, but his feelings were shared by many Swedish Americans at the time. Before his House term expired in 1917, Lindbergh made a final effort to halt a declaration of war by calling for a popular referendum on the issue. The final voting on the Armed Ships Bill in the House of Representatives demonstrated his isolated position in the Congress and spelled his political defeat. Lindbergh voted against the bill, but the House passed it by the overwhelming margin of 403 to 14.

In contrast to most Swedish Americans, Lindbergh stubbornly adhered to his convictions after America entered the war. Though now out of Congress, he brought his opinions to the attention of the American public by writing a book strongly critical of United States foreign policy. Running in the Republican primary for governor of Minnesota in 1918, Lindbergh was handed defeat by J. A. A. Burnquist, who came closer to matching the change in temperament among Swedish-American voters. Following the declaration of war, Burnquist became such an advocate of American nationalism that at one point he called for the deportation of all immigrants who could not speak English. During the last six years of his political career, ending in 1924. Lindbergh aligned himself with the Farmer-Labor party, which enjoyed a strong following among disgruntled Minnesota farmers and ranked as the third largest political party in the state. Lindbergh himself was never to return to Washington.

Out of the ranks of the Farmer-Labor party during the 1920s came another colorful politician of Scandinavian extraction, Floyd Bjornstjerne Olson, the son of a Norwegian father and a Swedish mother. Olson lost the state's gubernatorial election in 1924 as the Farmer-Labor candidate, but won a rematch six years later and held the governorship until his death in 1936. His political record gained him a reputation outside the state, and he was sometimes considered a more radical alternative to Franklin D. Roosevelt, even though Olson remained one of the president's staunchest supporters. As governor, Olson launched a vigorous campaign during the Great Depression for a comprehensive relief program and, with the help of farmers and industrial labor, saw to its passage. On the surface, at least, Olson's efforts are reminiscent of the Swedish Social Democrats' bargaining with the Farmers' party in 1933 to win a parliamentary majority for their own depression relief program.

In the long run Olson may have been too much of a liberal for the majority of Minnesota Swedes, and his outspoken prolabor sympathies in resolving industrial disputes lost him support among the state's farmers. Nevertheless, his alignment with the radical wing of the Democratic party is typical of the political sentiments of Scandinavian Minnesotans during this century. Even on the Republican side, many of them have championed the cause of progressive social legislation. While it is tempting to think that these developments owe some inspiration to the rapid progress of social democracy in Scandinavia, there is no direct evidence of this. Nearly all of Minnesota's leading Swedish-American politicians were born in this country, and it was here that their political ideals took shape. By the same token, their Swedish-American upbringing can hardly have been a working laboratory for radical political ideas brought to this country by their parents. The flight from political oppression was simply not a characteristic feature of Swedish emigration.

The danger in highlighting the achievements of prominent politicians from a certain immigrant group is that it can easily exaggerate the importance of the ethnic factor in American politics. Most politicians, including those of Swedish extraction, made a point of avoiding appeals to ethnic interests in their official campaign statements and public debates. On this level, then, there was no such thing as a dyed-in-the-wool Swedish or Scandinavian candidate, even if his name happened to be Lind, Johnson, Lindbergh or Olson. There were moments, however, during the last hectic days of an election campaign when candidates made an improvised bid for the ethnic vote and sometimes managed to win the necessary margin at the polls. A standard example of Scandinavian ethnicity in American elections is provided by J. A. Johnson's gubernatorial campaign of 1904. His unexpected victory in normally Republican territory is said to have been the result of ballot hopping by Scandinavian voters. Johnson received 25 percent of the votes from Swedish Republicans and 20 percent from Norwegian Republicans. Although his campaign personnel claimed that the election reflected the strength of Johnson's own personality, his ethnic background must have had an immediate impact and appeal among Scandinavian voters.

There is an obvious reason for giving exclusive coverage to

Along *Sillgatan* (Herring Street) in Gothenburg, the offices of the emigrant agencies were packed together like sardines.

Frederick Nelson.

Agent i Sverige:
J. O. Nelson, under firma
Frederick Nelson,
Skeppsbron.

Agent i Hull:
Walter Thomas.

Hufvud-Contor i
Liverpool.
23. Water Street 23.

№ 4525

UTVANDRARE-KONTRAKT,

upprättadt emellan **Frederick Nelson**, befullmäktigad utvandrings-agent enligt Lagen af den 5 Februari 1869, och nedanstående utvandrare:

Utvandrarens Namn.	Ålder.	Sednaste vistelseort.	Lägervitelse.
Christin Carlsson	25	Holland	Hisborg

Göteborg den 10 April 1872

Medicilahnse
General-Agent.

Upprättadt och godkändt såsom upprättadt i öfverenstämmelse med Kongl. Förords. l. 5 Februari 1869, betygas: Göteborg i Polishamn. 1 April 1872

An emigrant contract served as a travel document as well as a steamship ticket. In this case the fare from Gothenburg to New York was 132 *riksdaler* ($33).

Hans Mattson's advertisement for railroad land in the emigrant newspaper *Amerika* in 1872.

Posters of the Atlantic steamship lines brightened the drabness of everyday rural life, as in this interior from a Swedish cottage.

Swedish-American journalist Fritjof Colling (1863-1944), who ended his days as editor of *Hjo Tidning,* sketched the return of the native in a series of drawings, "Mr. Coleson's Trip to Sweden."

Castle Garden, located at the lower end of Manhattan Island, gave emigrants their first glimpse of America.

"Old Main" on the campus of Augustana College in Rock Island, Illinois.

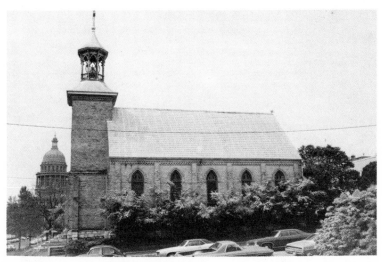

Typical of many churches built by Swedish immigrants, Gethsemane Lutheran Church in Austin, Texas, was erected in 1833 out of materials from the old state capitol. Design and labor were furnished by the members.

In an oil painting by Olof Krans, women at the Bishop Hill colony plant corn in rank, guided by the men at both ends of the rope.

The Bishop Hill Colony as painted by colonist Olof Krans.

the Minnesota side of Swedish-American politics. Minnesota is the one state in the Union where Swedes have commanded the center of attention. With two exceptions, all of the state's governors since 1905 have been Scandinavian born or of Scandinavian descent. No less than ten of the twenty-six American governors who have come from purely Swedish backgrounds have held office in Minnesota. Of the remaining sixteen a surprising total of three have served the governorship of Montana, a state with a very small Swedish population. Colorado and Nebraska have each elected two Swedish-American governors, and one has served in the states of California, Delaware, Idaho, Kansas, Michigan, Oregon, South Dakota, Vermont, and Washington. Strangely enough, Illinois is not on this list. As a rule, Swedish Americans have been more successful in running for public office in their home states than in making a breakthrough on the national scene. Twelve have been elected to the United States Senate, including three from Minnesota.

Despite their numbers, Swedish Americans had few representatives in public office during the early emigration period. This is not particularly surprising, as the immigrants' first decades in this country were filled with the practical tasks of adjusting to a new social and economic environment. In time some of them won election to local or municipal offices, especially in areas where Swedes represented a majority of the population. On the state and federal levels, however, developments came much later. It was not until the 1880s that Scandinavians as a whole became an important factor in state politics. The first evidence of this can be traced in Minnesota, where Scandinavians commanded a 36 percent share of the population. Their definite political breakthrough, on the other hand, came during this century. As far as Minnesota is concerned, Scandinavians have nearly been overrepresented in state government, while their representation in other states can be described as moderate to good. On the more specific issue of party affiliation, twentieth-century Swedish Americans resist an outright characterization. Differences of time and geography make it almost impossible to determine whether they have voted a primarily Republican or Democratic ticket.

Swedes in American Wars

Swedish immigrant involvement in American politics has some reflection on their participation in American wars since the start of the emigration era. Which side held their sympathies during the Civil War, and what were their feelings toward American involvement in World Wars I and II?

> To the Scandinavians of Minnesota!
> It is high time for us, as a people, to rise with sword in hand, and fight for our adopted country and for liberty. . . .
> Countrymen, "arise to arms; our adopted country calls!" Let us prove ourselves worthy of that land, and of those heroes from whom we descend. I hereby offer myself . . . and I am confident that many of you are ready and willing to do likewise. Let each settlement send forth its little squad.
>
> Hans Mattson's appeal in a Swedish-American newspaper, 1861.[1]

> We disagree with you on the slavery issue. We live in a slave state, have daily contact with slaves as well as slave owners, and are of the opinion that slaves receive better food, better treatment, and better respect than the working classes in Sweden.
>
> Letter from a Texas Swede to the Swedish-American newspaper, *Hemlandet,* in 1855.

Of these two quotations the second is least typical of Swedish-American opinion on the burning issue of slavery, which divided the Union and set an entire nation aflame. Research into the Confederate Army's muster rolls shows that approximately twenty-five Swedes fought on the southern side. The actual figure may have been higher, but it was nowhere near the number for the Union Army, in which over three thousand Swedes served. Swedish-American enthusiasm for the Union cause is illustrated by the fact that about half (thirteen hundred) of the nearly twenty-five hundred Illinois Swedes qualified for military service enlisted as volunteers. Hans Mattson's newspaper appeal in 1861 was crowned with immediate success, and he became the captain of an entire Scandinavian company that flew the colors of Minnesota's Third Volunteer Regiment and went by the nickname of "Hans Mattson's Scandinavian Guard." By the end of the Civil War, Mattson had risen to the rank of colonel. Documents from this period also show that the Union Army saw service by eleven other Swedish-born colonels and three brigadier generals.

During the two World Wars, most Swedish Americans adopted an isolationist position, which was often the prevailing ideology of the Republican party. Once it became clear that America could not afford to remain neutral, Swedes were forced to show their colors. It is probably correct that during the early years of World War I the average Swedish American was pro-German, but his sympathies in this respect were a direct inheritance of Sweden's age-old animosity toward arch-rival Imperial Russia. On the whole, Swedish Americans were more concerned about the fate of American neutrality than about the advantages of a military alliance between the United States and Germany.

In 1942 the American magazine *Fortune* offered the following assessment of Swedish-American sentiment after the American entrance into World War II: "Though interventionist Carl Sandburg is their greatest pride, the 1,400,000 first- and second-generation Swedes in the U. S. still stand for whatever is left of the Midwest's specific isolationism. Stronger only than their anti-Russian feeling is their ready understanding of Sweden's 'realistic' attempt to avoid Nazi invasion by voluntary, though limited, collaboration with the Reich."[2] The magazine article went on to describe Swedish Americans as decent, law-abiding citizens who did what was expected of them, but with little enthusiasm.

In the long run, however, Swedish Americans showed an unflagging loyalty to the Allied war effort, and they were every bit as concerned about its success as the rest of the American population. In fact, their sympathies gained a special focus as a result of Sweden's official policy of neutrality and its compromised relations with Germany after 1940.

The Swedish-American Press

Now more than a century old, the Swedish-American press traces its origins to a newspaper called *Skandinavien,* which began publication in New York in 1851. Though a short-lived experiment with an irregular printing schedule, *Skandinavien* still holds the distinction of being the first in a long line of Swedish-American newspapers. A successor of more consequence was *Hemlandet, Det Gamla och Det Nya* (The Old and the New Homeland), which started publication in Galesburg, Illinois, in 1855. Under the leadership of its publisher, T. N. Hasselquist, a local Swedish Lutheran minister and prominent Augustana Synod figure, *Hemlandet* rapidly became a forum for the Swedish Lutheran churches in this country. It was not until 1866 that the first independent Swedish newspaper rolled off the immigrant presses. *Svenska Amerikanaren* (The Swedish American) was established that year in Chicago as a deliberately liberal alternative to the growing ranks of denominational newspapers.

The subsequent history of the Swedish-American press, characterized by an endless series of title deaths and hopeful mergers, can only be sketched here. At the height of its development this immigrant press was represented in thirty different states across the country. In Minnesota alone no less than thirty separate towns and cities became centers of Swedish-American journalism. Today the picture is altogether different: of the approximately twelve hundred newspapers published since 1851, only seven remain.

The Swedish-American press experienced its greatest crisis during the years before and after World War I, when Americanization became a cultural watchword in immigrant circles. Subscription slumps and outright failures reaped a grim harvest on all sides, and for those who managed to survive, the halt of mass emigration in 1930 did the rest. Mergers provided only a temporary solution to a growing problem. Sixty years ago, before their merger, the two Chicago papers, *Svenska Amerikanaren* and *Svenska Tribunen-Nyheter* (The Swedish Tribune-News), enjoyed respective circulations of eighty thousand and seventy thousand. Today the average circulation of the entire Swedish-American press stands at approximately twenty-six thousand.

The reason for these developments is the decline of the Swedish language as a communication medium in American society. In the beginning the Swedish-American press drew its readership from first-generation immigrants who arrived in this country with little or no knowledge of English and depended upon Swedish-language newspapers as their major source of information about America. Even after they had become adjusted to American society and found time to learn English, they continued to turn to the immigrant press for news about their old home districts. This interest has not been shared by the second or third generations of Swedish Americans, who, in addition, have a poor reading knowledge of Swedish. As a result, the fate of these newspapers has largely paralleled the life stream of the first immigrant generation.

Aside from dispensing the latest news from Sweden, the Swedish-American press also fulfilled the function of preserving immigrant self-identity. Newspapers became a kind of family Bible, which recorded the births, marriages, deaths, and other notable events in the life of the Swedish-American population. The gradual assimilation of Swedish immigrants into American society, however, and the loss of this ethnic identity, have undermined the residual strength of this immigrant press.

According to available statistics, the largest of the six surviving Swedish newspapers is *Svenska Amerikanaren Tribunen* (Chicago) with a circulation of approximately nine thousand. Second largest is *Nordstjernan-Svea* (The North Star-Svea), founded in New York in 1872, with a current circulation of five thousand. West Coast newspapers consist of *California Veckoblad* (California Weekly), published in Los Angeles (average circulation twenty-eight hundred), and *Vestkusten* (the West Coast, approximately twelve hundred readers), a San Francisco hallmark since 1886, despite some typographical mishaps after the earthquake of 1906. Although the old Swedish settlements around Austin, Texas, have seen only a trickle of newcomers since their founding some one hundred years ago, they continue to publish a local paper called *Texas-Posten,* which has a current circulation of roughly one thousand. In Denver, Colorado, a family of Swedish printers manages the presses of the *Western News,* an exclusively English-language publication with a circulation of approximately one thousand. Both this paper and *Vest-kusten* are issued twice a month, while the rest are weeklies. With the exception of the *Western News* at least 50 percent of today's Swedish-American newspapers are published in Swedish. While *Svenska Amerikanaren Tribunen* is the only paper published by a non-Swede, it is printed entirely in Swedish.

With the passage of time and the changing needs of their readers, Swedish newspapers have assumed more of a unifying role in Swedish-American circles. Their major purpose today is to serve the organized interests of the Swedish community with news of club meetings and special events. In the process the Swedish language has given way to English as the primary medium of communication. For those with relatives and friends in Sweden, the Swedish-American press has a more personal, even sentimental value. Drawing on news releases from the Swedish Ministry of Foreign Affairs or clippings forwarded by newspapers around Sweden, the Swedish-American press supplies coverage of news developments in immigrants' home districts. The emphasis given to local-interest news reflects the intimate ties Swedish Americans have always had to their home provinces as opposed to Sweden as a whole. Certain newspapers, however, have gone one step further by stressing the need for a revival of interest in the Swedish language and Swedish culture.

What does the future hold for the Swedish-American press? A positive answer to this question depends largely upon the ability of these newspapers to reach the third and fourth generations of Swedish Americans, many of whom have begun to explore their Swedish heritage but want to know more about modern Sweden. They need current information in English, and if the Swedish-American press can fill this demand, it will not only rejuvenate itself but rescue a more than one hundred-year old publishing tradition from passing into oblivion.

Swedish-American Literature

If "writer's itch" ever became an affliction of Swedish immigrant culture, it probably reached a fever peak during the decades around the turn of the century, when the term "Swedish America" first entered the popular vocabulary. Evidence of this is found in journalist Ernst Skarstedt's classic study from 1897, *Våra Pennfäktare* (Our Ink-Slingers), which contains the biographies of over three hundred Swedish-American writers. Nearly all of them were Swedish-born, and their literary style, especially on the lyrical side, reflected the prevailing trends in Sweden at the time of their emigration. This meant that Swedish-American poetry always lagged a bit behind developments on the other side of the Atlantic.

Religious themes lay at the heart of much of this writing and often echoed the romantic nationalism of eighteenth- and early nineteenth-century Swedish literature, with its heady strains of Nordic mythology. Pastoral or nature poetry was preoccupied with descriptions of Swedish forests, lakes, and meadows and came to epitomize the immigrants' nostalgic picture of Swedish provincial life. The same images were used to highlight the special virtues of Nordic culture and their ennobled transplantation to the new continent by Swedish Americans. Idealism ran rampant, as illustrated by the following lines from Ludwig Holmes' poem "Till Studenter" (To Students):

> stor är svensken icke blott i strid,
> på andra fält han äfven segrar vann,
> och främst han står i bildning, kraft och id
> och bryter väg, där förr man väg ej fann.

As warrior bold the Swede responds when summoned forth to strife,
As victor yet his fame extends to other realms of life.
With feats of wisdom, prowess, pluck he does the world astound,
And blazes trails where once no trace of mankind's step was found.[3]

Some lyricists broke with these traditions and turned to America for a new source of inspiration. Magnus Elmblad's poem "Den fjärde juli" (The Fourth of July) offers one example:

Ingen boja här din tanke fjettrar,
Om du sjelf ej bojor bära vill.
Intet kyrkoråd din tro förkättar,
Om du sjelf ej, ljusskygg, hjelper till.
Ingen stormans röst vid valet väger
Mer än din—om du begagnar den.
Vill du frihet, frihet ock du eger,
Kan gå trygg och nöjd bland fria män.

No chains in this land shackle any man's thought,
Lest you forge the iron with which they are wrought.
No church council bans your creed or belief,
Lest you acquiesce in timid relief.
No rich man's vote counts more at the poll,
Lest you throw yours away or never enroll.
If it's freedom you want, it is yours without flaw,
For you live among free men, where respect is the law.[4]

The sentiments expressed in this poem pose an interesting contrast to one of Elmblad's famous ballads, "Petter Jönssons Resa till Amerika" (Peter Jönssons Voyage to America), which was originally published in *Svenska Amerikanaren* in November, 1872. In this work Elmblad satirizes the average Swede's decision to emigrate. An avid reader of the popular Swedish newspaper *Fäderneslandet* (The Fatherland), which among the upper classes was considered a haven for radical opinion, Petter Jönsson is led to believe that Sweden has fallen into the destructive hands of a civil bureaucracy and that his worst enemies are the priest and local sheriff. Apart from his naïve acceptance of newspaper editorials, Jönsson has a simplistic faith in America's golden opportunities, which loom in his eyes as a paradise of idle hours, a steady supply of meat and potatoes, and an oasis of boot polish. Putting two and two together, Jönsson sets about planning his trip to America.

This, at any rate, is Elmblad's view of the decision-making process among the Swedish lower classes, and as such it characterizes the highbrow mentality of Uppsala University students and other conservative Swedish circles. Elmblad wrote his ballad only a year after his arrival in this country, which followed a few terms of study in Uppsala. He shared the belief that the Swedish lower classes were "betraying" their country by emigrating to America and, like his contemporaries, blamed left-wing political circles for their exaggerated criticism of Swedish society. When "The Fourth of July" was published, Elmblad happened to be on the editorial staff of *Svenska Amerikanaren,* a paper that took every opportunity to criticize conditions in Swedish society. By this time Petter Jönsson's cause was also Elmblad's: Sweden had fallen prey to the bureaucrats, and there was good reason to emigrate. Between these two poems, then, lies the true-to-life odyssey of a Swedish immigrant, the Uppsala student turned Swedish American.

One of the more distinguishing themes of Swedish-American prose literature was the return visit to Sweden, with its mixture of nostalgia and surprise. While the lyricists usually portrayed Sweden as the haven for homesick emigrants, prose authors made an effort to depict the changes that had taken place, for better or for worse, since their departure. A "bird of a slightly different feather" was humorist Frithiof Colling's *Mister Colesons Sverigeresa* (Mister Coleson's Trip to Sweden), published in Minneapolis in 1896 under the pen name of Gabriel Carlson. While Colling poked fun at the stereotype Swedish American, who constantly amazed the people back home with his flashy clothes and exaggerated airs, he painted a sympathetic picture of Mr. Coleson's exasperating reencounter with stodgy, class-minded Swedish society.

The concepts of ethnic identity and immigrant self-image won recognition from authors on both sides of the Swedish-American literary front, but particularly from commentators on immigrant life and culture. Countless volumes were written near the turn of the century about the history and achievements of Swedish settlers in various states, although at times the economics of publishing clouded the real purpose of their publication. Many of these works were financed on a subscription basis and tended to highlight the more successful members of the immigrant community, who had paid for and often written their own biographies.

Swedish-American prose also has its romantic or nostalgic elements, represented by the scores of novels and short stories depicting the American immigrant experience. Many authors saw the assimilation process and the immigrant success story in terms of a loss of identity and the destruction of moral fibre. The American urban environment symbolized both decay and despair and stood in sharp contrast to the healthy cultural surroundings Swedish Americans had left behind, either in Sweden or in the rural Middle West.

In his recent study of Swedish-American language patterns, Nils Hasselmo presents some interesting statistics on the production of Swedish-American fiction in book format between 1865 and 1955. Drawing on O. Fritiof Ander's selective bibliography of 1956, Hasselmo finds that few literary works left the presses of immigrant publishers during the first twenty-year period, 1865–85. Only nine book titles were issued during the initial production spurt between 1876 and 1880. The first real production peak was reached from 1891 to 1895 (twenty-eight titles), and the second from 1906 to 1910 (twenty-nine titles). An average of roughly twenty-three book titles left the presses of Swedish-American publishing houses during each five-year period from 1885 to 1910. Book production reached its peak from 1911 to 1915, with a total of fifty-one titles, but dropped to thirty titles from 1916 to 1920. Publication continued to decline during the 1920s and ebbed by the mid-1930s. No more than six Swedish-language book titles were issued by Swedish-American publishing houses between 1941 and 1955. As all of these statistics pertain to book publishing, however, they account for only one-half of the Swedish-American authors on the publishing scene.

In other words, book statistics do not tell the whole story. The vast majority of Swedish-American poets and prose authors turned to periodical publications—newspapers, literary magazines, and annual calendars—as their primary means of communication. At times, however, the ethnic press promoted the distribution of Swedish books by offering them as incentives or premiums to new subscribers.

The rise of a distinctive Swedish-American literature during the late 1880s enhanced the vitality of the Swedish language among immigrant writers and publishers. During World War I, however, English-language titles began to compete with the Swedish, and by the 1920s they had taken the upper hand. After 1937 the Augustana Lutheran Book Concern discontinued publication of all Swedish-language materials, except for a few Swedish textbooks and magazines. It is somewhat ironical that of all the publications issued by immigrant publishing houses, songbooks have played the greatest role in prolonging the life of the Swedish language. The Augustana Book Concern began its English-language production with the publication of a Swedish-American songbook where, for the very first time, the English text stood side by side with the Swedish.

At time wore on, more and more Swedish-American authors began to publish in both languages. Some of them, such as G. N. Malm, addressed themselves to immigrant readers even when writing in English. On the whole, however, those who wrote in English did so neither as Swedish Americans nor as cultivators of a Swedish-American reading public. The language transition symbolized, in effect, the ultimate assimilation of Swedish-language authors to American society and the loss of a distinct ethnic profile. A prime example of this is found in Carl Sandburg, perhaps the first great Swedish-American author, whose poetry expresses an altogether nonethnic orientation.

Swedish-American Church Life

Methodists and Baptists, the largest denominations on the American frontier, won many new members among immigrant Swedes, especially in Illinois. Much of this was due to the efforts of Olof Gustaf Hedström, a former tailor from Kronobergs *län* in Småland, who in the early 1840s established a Methodist chapel aboard the "Bethel Ship John Wesley," anchored in New York harbor. Together with his brother Jonas, who had settled in Illinois, Olof led the conversion of Swedish immigrants to the Methodist faith and directed their steps to the infant Swedish colonies in Illinois. In 1846 Jonas Hedström organized the Midwest's first Swedish Methodist congregation in Victoria, Illinois.

The pioneering figure among Swedish-American Baptists was Gustaf Palmquist, a former school teacher from Gustavsberg, who fell under the influence of Methodist preacher George S. Scott and Swedish evangelist Carl Olof Rosenius in Stockholm and emigrated for the purpose of spreading the gospel among Swedish Americans. After his arrival in Illinois, Palmquist became a Baptist convert and founded America's first Swedish Baptist congregation in Rock Island in 1852. Another denominational leader was Anders Wiberg, originally a priest in the State Lutheran Church but later a Baptist convert and, for a time, active among Swedish Americans.

Swedish-American Lutherans retained more of their ties with Sweden than their free-church brethren largely as a result of emigration by state church clergy. Emigration was the proper word for it, because there was no organized transplantation of Swedish Lutheran congregations to the American frontier. Once the state church had levelled its judgment on those who decided to emigrate, it more or less washed its hands of the matter and paid them little attention. Some of these emigrants were Lutheran clergymen who, because of their pietistic sympathies or associations with the temperance movement, had fallen out of grace with the church hierarchy, and they became the leaders of the new Lutheran congregations in America. The pioneer was Lars Paul Esbjörn, a former priest from Oslättsfors in Gästrikland, who emigrated in 1849 along with a group of Lutheran pietists from Hälsingland. In 1850 Esbjörn established a Swedish Lutheran congregation in Andover, Illinois, but spent the next few years as a circuit rider—preaching and raising money for his first church. Some of his travels took him to the East, and during his stay in Boston, Esbjörn received a donation of $1,500 from Jenny Lind, the Swedish concert singer. In 1854 the Andover church was ready for consecration.

Esbjörn's indefatigable energy inspired other immigrant Lutheran clergy and led to the founding of Lutheran congregations throughout the Middle West. In 1860 the Augustana Synod was born from the merger of thirty-six Swedish congregations and their Norwegian brethren. Swedes and Norwegians did not always see eye to eye on religious issues or the affairs of their home countries, and in 1870 the Norwegians withdrew from the synod to form one of their own.

The Augustana Synod eventually became the largest Swedish-American denomination. At the time of its founding in 1860, it had 43 congregations and represented approximately 20 percent of the Swedish-American population. In 1910, at the time of its greatest relative expansion, the synod had over 1,000 congregations serving more than one-third of the Swedish-American population. Two decades later, in 1930, the synod's membership stood at a peak of 250,000, served by 856 active ministers in over 1,200 congregations across the country.

The small congregations established by the four "patriarchs"—Esbjörn, T. N. Hasselquist, Erland Carlsson, and Erik Norelius—had very primitive beginnings. In fact, the evangelical background of their founders, coupled with the prayer-meeting spirit of the earliest gatherings, had much in common with the private devotional services among the early Swedish pietists. Once a congregation had secured its own pastor, it began building its first church, usually a simple log structure with pews and a pulpit. The next step was an historic one in the life of every Swedish settlement—the consecration of a frame church, crowned by a bell tower, in imitation of those in the Swedish countryside. Today the churches of the Augustana Synod have few similarities with the early congregations, and their pietistic flavor has steadily diminished.

The second largest Swedish-American denomination, after the Augustana Synod, was the Swedish Evangelical Covenant, which in 1930 had thirty thousand members. Like the Augustana Lutherans, the Covenanters (or Mission Friends) developed as a pietist reaction to the conservative Lutheran state church. Led by the dynamic P. P. Waldenström, they established themselves as an independent body in 1878. The first Covenanters who emigrated to America joined the Augustana Synod, but even here there was friction between orthodox and evangelical sentiment, and during the 1860s many Mission Friends withdrew to form their own congregations. In 1885 the Swedish Evangelical Mission Covenant became a reality. One of its leaders was E. A. Skogsbergh, who served as pastor of the Minneapolis church from 1884–1908 and became one of the outstanding preachers in Swedish-American circles.

Swedish-American Methodists and Baptists did not share the same close ties to organized Swedish church life as the Augustana Synod and the Mission Covenant. Instead, their formative development took place in this country, after emigration, and built upon the missionary efforts of American preachers in Sweden. In time both groups founded special Swedish conferences under the auspices of the American Methodist and Baptist denominations.

From the very beginning all of these churches adopted Swedish as their official language, but with the passage of time the language question became a highly divisive issue. Before the mass immigration surge of the 1880s, it presented no real problem, as everyone was convinced that English would inevitably replace Swedish in the context of religious worship. By the turn of the century, however, America had become the home of one out of every five Swedes, and the tide of opinion changed dramatically. The majority of Swedish-American churchgoers now wanted to retain Swedish, maintaining that it had become synonymous with their Christian faith. Swedish was not only a "holy language" but the indispensable medium of Swedish-American worship. This majority opinion was opposed by strong voices in every denomination who advocated that the transition to English safeguarded the future of Swedish-American church life. It was obvious to them that if the churches were to attract the second and third immigrant generations, most of whom had a poor knowledge of Swedish and had entered the mainstream of American society, they ought to concern themselves more about declining membership than the longevity of a minority language.

The struggle between these two factions was bitter and reached a peak between 1900 and 1914. The churches themselves, however, never managed to resolve their differences, and in the final analysis Swedish died out as a result of external pressures. World War I was the turning point in the life of the Swedish language. It not only signaled the end of steady immigration by non-English-speaking Swedes, but also created a social climate in which Americans as well as immigrants looked with suspicion on non-American organizations, cultures, and languages.

One of the first victims of the Americanization campaign was the ethnic press, which saw its readership drift away to English-language papers. In time English also made inroads on the associative life of the Swedish immigrant community: clubs, lodges, and societies abandoned Swedish in their official record keeping. One by one the Swedish-American churches followed suit, although the transition was hardly noticeable at first. The experiment with religious services in both languages, however, set an irrevocable trend, and within a short time Swedish had been forced out of the churches.

In 1924 the minutes of the Augustana Synod's general assembly were printed for the first time in English; one year later the synod received its first English-language order of worship. The Association of English Churches, which since 1908 had represented the interests of the English-language minority in the synod, was dissolved in 1931 for the simple reason that it was no longer needed. Instead, a new organization was established to protect the interests of the Swedish-language congregations, which were becoming fewer and fewer all the time. By the mid-1930s English had become the official language of the Augustana Synod, and in 1962 the synod entered into the merger now known as the Lutheran Church of America.

The same fate awaited the Swedish language in other immigrant churches. Led by its strong, pro-Swedish clergy, the Swedish Evangelical Mission Covenant offered stiff resistance to the Americanization process, but at the end of the 1920s English was adopted as its official language. In 1933 the annual minutes were printed for the first time in English, and in 1937 the word *Swedish* disappeared from the church's title. Despite these developments, the Covenant has maintained its contacts with its Swedish heritage.

The language question posed an even greater threat to Swedish-American Baptists and Methodists, which were formally a part of American denominations. They realized that once the Swedish language had disappeared from their services, their special identity would be lost, and they might have no other alternative than to be totally absorbed by their American counterparts. This possibility revitalized efforts to maintain a distinct ethnic profile, and to some extent they managed to hold out against the tide. Swedish Methodist conferences in the Middle West and East survived until the early 1940s, when they dropped their special jurisdictional boundaries within the Methodist connection. The Swedish Baptists, however, had theological reasons for continuing as an independent national body; they dropped the word *Swedish,* and became known as the Baptist General Conference of America, welcoming into their membership other Baptist churches without regard to ethnic origin.

Swedish-American Education

Swedish-American churches often took the initiative in establishing schools on the American frontier, and even after the opening of public schools they continued to provide children with religious education and systematic instruction in Swedish. English, of course, was the official classroom language in public schools, and in predominently Swedish communities this created problems for public school teachers who, despite their own Swedish heritage, had the responsibility of introducing English to their pupils. In some cases pupils who used the recess period as an opportunity to lapse into Swedish were told to remain in their seats at the end of the day. The negative experiences shared by many second-generation Swedish Americans during the early school years, especially the heckling from the English-speaking majority, doubtlessly explains a good deal of their disenchantment with the Swedish language.

Between 1910 and 1917 some American high schools introduced Scandinavian-language courses into their curriculum. In 1912, for example, no less than 45 schools across the country offered such instruction, more than half of which (26) were located in Minnesota. In 1917 the figure had reached a total of 63 schools, and enrollment in Swedish-language courses alone accounted for 1,822 students. That was both the height and the end of the experiment. After America's entrance into World War I, foreign-language courses fell into disrepute and many were banned. Ten years later 65 percent of the schools that originally offered Swedish-language courses had removed them from the curriculum. Enrollment had dropped by 75 percent.

Despite the immigration of Swedish Lutheran clergy, the Augustana Synod soon found itself with a shortage of available ministers, and it was only a matter of time before it took steps to establish its own theological seminary. As early as 1858 Lars Paul Esbjörn began training Scandinavian immigrants for the Lutheran ministry at Illinois State University in Springfield, where he held a professorship in "Scandinavian languages, chemistry, astronomy, *etc., etc.*" In 1860, following a dispute with the university administration, Esbjörn moved the Scandinavian department to Chicago, which became the site of Augustana College and Seminary. Two years later he embarked on a fund-raising campaign to Sweden but never returned, and his responsibilities were assumed by T. N. Hasselquist, the first president of the Augustana Synod. Hasselquist soon moved the college and its seminary to the small community of Paxton, south of Chicago. This new location proved to be a move in the wrong direction, for Paxton was an isolated small town on the Illinois prairie and hardly enhanced the college's development. In 1875 the synod chose Rock Island, Illinois, as the official site of its new campus. Today Augustana College has grown in size and reputation, and a large part of its student body of approximately twenty-two hundred can claim Swedish background. The Seminary became an independent institution and was moved to Chicago in 1967 as part of the Lutheran School of Theology at Chicago, which is the training center of the Lutheran Church in America.

Theological education was also a major concern of other Swedish-American denominations, and they soon followed suit with their own seminaries, which eventually blossomed into undergraduate colleges. The Mission Covenant established North Park College and Seminary in Chicago. The Swedish Baptists offered theological courses through an American theological seminary (later the Divinity School of the University of Chicago) before merging their program in 1914 with Bethel Academy in Minneapolis to form Bethel College and Seminary. The first Swedish Methodist seminary was opened in Galesburg, Illinois, but was later moved to Evanston, where it developed into a junior college (Evanston Collegiate Institute) in 1934 and was renamed Kendall College in 1950.

Some regional conferences of the Augustana Synod founded their own institutions of higher education. Examples include Gustavus Adolphus College in Minnesota, Bethany College in Kansas, Luther College in Nebraska, and Upsala College in New Jersey. Although all of them have entered the mainstream of American higher education they still retain their Swedish flavor, and over the years they have symbolized a positive force in the assimilation of Swedish immigrants and their children.

As the theological seminaries branched out into under-graduate colleges, the Swedish language lost its privileged status in classroom instruction. English usually made its first inroads by the end of the first decade, primarily in such subjects as history and the natural sciences. As time went by Swedish was forced to retreat to its traditional bulwark, theology and religious educa-tion. By the 1930s its fate was sealed, and it shared the same status as any other foreign language.

Swedish-American Organizations

There is a great deal of truth to the statement that whenever they settled, Swedish immigrants had a knack for organizing themselves into a myriad of religious, cultural, and fraternal circles. Ethnic identity and the desire for cultural self-maintenance found vibrant expression among immigrant en-claves in American cities, where rural immigrants in particular faced a new and sometimes frightening environment. In the beginning the church stood at the hub of all immigrant activity, both in rural and urban areas. As conditions normalized and the enclaves assumed a character of their own, a rich flora of secular organizations emerged on the scene. Chicago alone had more than seventy different Swedish clubs and societies during the course of the 1870s; many of them drew their membership from specific Swedish provinces or districts. Although their purpose and format varied as much as immigrants' needs and interests, the majority had the character of temperance lodges, choral societies, gymnastic clubs and fraternal orders. Many of them also fulfilled the function of benevolent or immigrant self-help associations by providing sick- or death-benefit insurance for paying members. In many cases the selection of an organizational title highlighted the desire to maintain contacts with Swedish culture and history. Names such as "Svea," "Svithiod," and "Viking" captured the mood of the old Nordic sagas and echoed the strains of romantic nationalism in Swedish literature and the fine arts.

Many of these local societies eventually joined forces with national federations, of which the largest were the Vasa Order of America, founded in Connecticut in 1896; the Independent Order of Vikings, established in Chicago in 1890; and the Independent Order of Svithiod, another Chicago hallmark from 1880. Their initial purpose was immigrant self-help based on a system of sick- and death-benefit insurance premiums. The charter of the Vasa Order, for example, included the following objectives: "To render aid to sick members of the corporation, whether such sickness be temporary or incurable, and to render pecuniary aid towards defraying the funeral expenses of members, and to promote social and intellectual fellowship among its members." With the passage of time these three Swedish-American orders have focused their attention more on the preservation of Swedish cultural traditions than on benevolent programs for members, and "social and intellectual fellowship" has come to include extension of contacts with the old country. Consequently, although they continue to operate Swedish retirement homes and hospitals, most of their activities center around language courses, Swedish history classes, folk dancing, and concerts of Swedish music. At the height of Swedish-American culture in 1929, the Vasa Order of America had seventy-two thousand members. Today its membership stands at thirty-eight thousand and is spread among three hundred sixty local lodges, of which five thousand members represent the fifty affiliate lodges in Sweden.

As a rule, Swedes did not develop any interest in the early history of their native country or its cultural memories until after they arrived in America. Most of them had never had the benefits of a secondary education in Sweden, and therefore their appreciation of Swedish history had little in common with the lofty patriotism of certain segments of the Swedish population, which were constantly celebrating the nation's "manifest destiny." In fact, these were the same people who stood in the front line of opposition to emigration and denounced all emigrants as traitors to the national heritage.

Once they arrived in this country, Swedes found themselves surrounded by nationalistic feelings. Part of this stemmed from America's own rise to world prominence around the turn of the century and part from the vibrant current of ethnic pride among other European immigrant groups. It was only natural, then, that Swedes developed their own sense of nationalism, which combined a nostalgia for the good, simple life back home with romantic pride in the great events of Swedish history. Although this blossomed at times into full-fledged American patriotism, the ground swell came from the immigrants' own concept of self-worth and the belief that they were transplanting the best virtues of Swedish or Scandinavian culture onto American soil. Such feelings frequently found their way into speeches and oratory held at Swedish-American gatherings. On one occasion in Minnesota the venerable Hans Mattson concluded his speech with the following words: "Only as a *united* people will we improve our chances of transplanting the virtues we have inherited from our beloved home provinces. A century from now posterity will be able to point with pride to all of the noble, worthy virtues of the Scandinavian nationalities in this, the largest, noblest nation in human history—the American nation, . . . and future generations will, until the end of time, hail the achievements of nineteenth-century Scandinavians in America.[5] Mattson's speech is typical of the vivid Pan-Scandinavian sentiments uttered on ceremonial occasions. On a day-to-day basis, however, Scandinavian immigrants were far less idealistic and often clashed bitterly in the political arena and the columns of the ethnic press.

During the immigration period, other tensions arose between the religious and secular societies, primarily those in urban areas. Much of this was rooted in contrasting social backgrounds, which contained overtones of a class struggle. The average Swedish immigrant who broke away from rural surroundings to settle in cities such as Chicago was generally inclined to join the Augustana Lutheran Synod, whose charitable societies, schools, and hospitals stood at his disposal. Those who came from urbanized areas and represented either the Swedish middle or, as in a few isolated cases, upper classes were far more likely to join the secular societies, which offered a tantalizing array of cultural and sociable entertainment—concerts, plays, balls, outings, and the like. The friction between these two groups was especially bitter in the Chicago enclaves. Followers of the Augustana Synod accused the secular societies of being the offshoots of Swedish middle-class culture, while the societies expressed their disgust with what they termed the intolerant spirit of the synod. Similar tensions developed out of the assimilation process and cast a shadow on immigrant church life. In the beginning the members of both the Augustana Lutheran and the free churches had a lower social standing than the rest of the American churchgoing population. As immigrants began to climb the social ladder or to make careers for themselves in particular professions, some of them broke away from their original surroundings to join more distinguished or "high church" circles, such as the American Episcopal Church.

9   Americanization

Many of America's immigrant groups, including the Swedes, have tended to pride themselves on their rapid assimilation to American life and culture. Researchers have approached the matter from a number of angles, and their findings challenge the validity of these claims. If, as sociologists maintain, intermarriage, or marriage between ethnic groups, is one reliable measurement of the assimilation process, then Swedish Americans have been slow to adjust to their new surroundings. Studies of Swedish settlements in rural and urban areas during the early and mass emigration periods indicate a decidedly low degree of intermarriage among first- and second-generation Swedish immigrants. In cases where intermarriage did take place, Swedes preferred to marry other Scandinavians, primarily Norwegians.

The language barrier itself had a negative influence on the inclination for intermarriage, and evidence of this can also be found among Swedish Americans. Those employed as office workers, store clerks, and toolmakers had the greatest tendency to intermarry, largely because their jobs demanded a ready knowledge of English.

Naturalization, the official entrance of new citizens into American society, provides researchers with another measurement of the internal dynamics in the adjustment process. Immigrants were entitled to become citizens after five years' residence, but could declare their intentions after only two years by filing their first papers. Most immigrants tended to postpone the final step toward naturalization, and the Swedes were no exception, even though they ranked among the leading groups of naturalized citizens from 1910 on. By this time, however, the peak decades of mass Swedish emigration were a part of history, and many of those who took the occasion to file their final naturalization papers had resided in this country well beyond the necessary five years.

While naturalization statistics provide a neat, generalized picture of ethnic groups in transition, they do not always tell the story of the individual immigrant. Research has found, for example, that the choice of settlement areas and occupations tended to have an impact on the citizen-making process. Immigrants in rural areas were apparently more eager to file their final papers than their urban countrymen. Among professional groups, well-educated immigrants led the ranks of new citizens, followed by lower civil-service employees, skilled workers, and, at the bottom of the scale, unskilled labor.

The vast majority of Swedish immigrants arrived in this country with little or no knowledge of English, and for them the language barrier spelled the difference between a rapid and torturously slow pace of assimilation. One can easily understand the pride they took in demonstrating their progress with the language, as evidenced by the somewhat confusing letters they sent to friends and relatives back home. For some sectors of the Swedish-American population, the language barrier was a natural check on the demands for rapid assimilation. The Augustana Synod and its ideological ally, the newspaper *Hemlandet,* were staunch advocates of Swedish-American nationalism and took every occasion to denounce the zealots of Americanization. The Swedish language held the key to the preservation of immigrant culture and assured the development of the synod's own educational programs. On the other side of the fence stood *Hemlandet's* arch-rival, the liberal *Svenska Amerikanaren,* which constantly stressed the necessity of learning English and adjusting to the demands of American society.

Despite the immigrants' eagerness to learn, the transition between languages and cultures was often slow and led to feelings of isolation, particularly when immigrants went to work in American homes and industries. While some of these feelings found their way into "America letters," many others were committed to memory and became the stories immigrants told about themselves decades later. In 1914, for example, a Halland emigrant went to work on a vegetable farm outside Providence, Rhode Island, where his brother had settled some years earlier. On a return visit to Sweden in 1968, this former emigrant gave the following description of his first encounter with the English language. "There were six of us Swedish greenhorns and 72 old Italian women working on that farm. Every night, when I came home to my brother's house, I thought I had added a new English word to my vocabulary, but most of the time it turned out to be an Italian swearword."[1]

The language transition also left its mark on immigrant family life, where the husband was customarily the major breadwinner and therefore had daily contact with Anglo-Americans. He became the family's first bilingual speaker, using English or "Swinglish" at his place of work and Swedish at home, among friends, in church, or at club meetings. This inevitably created problems for his children, who became the targets of name-calling at school and on public playgrounds. The risk of being called "squarehead" or "dumb Swede" forced many of them to disguise their nationality as best they could, to suppress their knowledge of Swedish, and to melt in with the rest of their schoolmates as 100 percent Americans. Swedish immigrant wives and mothers did not have the same range of contacts with the English-speaking world as their husbands or children and often suffered from acute isolation. At times family tensions gave way to feelings of outright anguish, especially when Swedish-speaking mothers discovered they were no longer able to communicate with their children or grandchildren.

There were, of course, cases where the situation was exactly the opposite. Before their marriage many immigrant housewives worked as maids in American homes, which provided ample opportunities for contacts with the English language and its native speakers. As a result, they were better equipped to meet the challenges of Americanization than their husbands, who had worked as farmhands, lumberjacks, and railroad workers in the nearly exclusive company of other Swedes or other immigrants.

The assimilation process met with some resistance in rural areas where Swedes had settled as compact enclaves and lived apart from the outside world. Here the Swedish language and customs retained more of their vitality, and the demands for rapid assimilation were much weaker. At times, however, the same sense of ethnic identity enabled urban Swedish immigrants to hold out against the tide of Americanization. Chicago can serve as one example.

The successive relocation of the Chicago Swedish enclaves during the 1800s was accompanied by changes in the immigrants' social and economic standards. During the squatter period of the 1840s and 1850s when Swedes settled along the north shore of the Chicago River, the major concern was survival. Many were without steady jobs, and countless others stayed only long enough to gain their bearings or earn enough money for a railroad ticket west. All of these conditions meant that life in the earliest Swedish enclave was highly unstable and unencouraging for further settlement.

Spurred by the prospects of steady jobs and private homes Swedes began to resettle during the 1860s along Chicago Avenue, which at that time was a center of German immigration. Though other nationalities filtered into the area, the Swedes soon established themselves as a distinct and highly stabilized enclave. Benevolent organizations, fraternal lodges, and other social gatherings turned Chicago Avenue into a bastion of Swedish culture and laid the groundwork for the rise of an ethnic press, the regular celebration of Swedish holidays, and the erection of such Chicago landmarks as the Linné statue. This outward display of ethnic solidarity was reinforced among families and private households, whose custom of accepting lodgers and boarders attracted scores of newcomers and gave the area all of the character of a genuine Swede Town.

By the 1890s conditions in Swede Town had deteriorated. Waves of new arrivals from non-Protestant countries of southern and eastern Europe forced many Swede Town residents to move to the suburbs, where living patterns and neighbors were conspicuously American. As Swedes began to climb the social and economic ladder, they dropped their attachments to the immigrant churches and cultural societies and looked to their new surroundings as a source of contacts and social norms. This signaled the end of the old Swedish neighborhoods and marked the final stage in the process of Americanization.

The assimilation process affected Swedes in different ways and with varying intensities. Some were forced to adjust rather quickly as a result of having skilled employment. Others managed to ease their way into American society by relying on a close circle of friends and the organized life of the immigrant community. For those in rural areas the tempo of assimilation was even slower, due largely to the homogeneous character of the earlier settlements and their isolation from the outside world. Despite these contrasts, the Swedes' adjustment to American society followed exactly the same pattern as that of all other non-English-speaking immigrants from northern Europe, with the possible exception of the Finns. On the whole, Swedes have not felt any great need to maintain a distinct ethnic profile on a more than local basis, and few of their churches and fraternal orders, despite what was said above, have developed significantly along regional or national lines.

There were times during the early part of this century, however, when Swedes did lay claim to a distinct indentity and raised the cry of ethnic solidarity. The outbreak of World War I was one of these reawakenings, although it eventually forced Swedes to display their loyalty to their new country. During the early years of the war the Swedish-American population was considered a hotbed of pro-German sympathies or, at best, a haven of isolationist sentiment, and the Swedish press did little to dispel these suspicions among the American public. America's entrance into the war challenged immigrants to show their true colors, and the Swedish-American press followed suit with a barrage of advertisements for Liberty Bonds. Typically enough, this sales campaign called more attention to the public image of Swedish Americans than to the bonds' importance in the war effort. Another reawakening of Swedish immigrant solidarity followed the passage of immigrant quota laws during the 1920s, when Swedes joined other nationalities in protesting these restrictions on unlimited immigration. In its own way the depression of the 1930s regalvanized the Swedish-American population and stimulated relief programs among needy countrymen.

In the final analysis none of these efforts was able to curb or even prolong the Americanization process. The Swedish-American press continued to lose readers, and the Swedish language disappeared from the churches and official record keeping. By the end of the 1930s, Swedes had become a definite part of American society.

While the same holds true today, much of the Swedish-American past lives on as a "secondary ethnicity" among older and younger immigrant generations. Many have begun to reexplore their heritage as a result of the New Ethnicity movement since the mid-1960s, which has challenged the popular belief that America's immigrants emerged from the melting pot as totally refined products. While "Swedish-American Power" may be generating a new wave of lapel buttons and bumper stickers, it lacks the dynamic elements present in other immigrant cultures which have turned such slogans into unique ethnic symbols.

Nevertheless, the interest in the cultural heritage of the Swedish immigrant is alive and growing, especially among American college and university students who have developed a taste for courses in the Swedish language, Swedish literature, films, music, politics, and social policy making. In many respects modern Sweden has become a new source of identity for these third- and fourth-generation Swedish Americans as well as a whetting stone for students' understanding of American society and their involvement in movements for social change. Much of this is reflected by the enrollment pattern at Scandinavian departments throughout the United States, where the majority of the approximately five thousand students come from non-Scandinavian backgrounds.

10 The Consequences of Emigration in Sweden

A study of the impact emigration had on Swedish society demands attention to a whole range of questions—economic, social, political, cultural, religious, and others. A central question, however, concerns the official attitude toward emigration on the part of Swedish lawmakers and the ruling classes.

Emigration was restricted by law as early as 1739. At that time the Swedish economy was in the hands of mercantile interests who were alarmed by the acute shortage of manpower in commerce and agriculture. The immediate purpose of this restrictive legislation, then, was to ensure the strength of the nation's economy and the expansion of its labor force. In 1840 a new law entitled Swedish citizens to emigrate without royal permission. This piece of legislation was entirely the result of liberal political opinion in Sweden and had no connection with the early trickle of emigration to America. From that point on the only persons restricted in their movements were military conscripts, who had to apply for royal permission to leave the country. The major purpose of supplementary legislation during the rest of the 1800s was to protect unsuspecting emigrants from exploitation at the hands of commercial and transport interests.

Laws and promulgations were one thing, public opinion another. Throughout the mass-emigration era, the Swedish ruling classes were strongly opposed to the idea and practice of emigration. In 1865, for example, the provincial governors and State clergymen circulated an official declaration in which they

132

warned the population of the consequences of emigration. Five years later, in the summer of 1870, Sweden's *chargé d'affaires* in Washington, Carl Lewenhaupt, was sent on a fact-finding tour of the Swedish settlements in the Middle West. The substance of his report, later published by the Swedish government, was more optimistic than anyone had anticipated. Lewenhaupt was particularly impressed by the progress since the 1850s, and he had nothing but praise for the material welfare of Swedish farmers and homesteaders. In the long run this fact-finding tour defeated the purpose of its original drafters, while gladdening the hearts of immigration supporters. The reaction of the American minister in Stockholm was typical: "The spirit of the report appears to me to be excellent."[1]

In Sweden the emigration issue divided public opinion into two camps, each of which developed its own arguments and solutions. The conservatives and ultranationalists opposed emigration for its damaging impact on the Swedish economy, particularly the manpower drain in agriculture, as well as for its depletion of a standing army based on military conscription. In their opinion, emigration was just as harmful to the national welfare as a general spirit of insubordination and a lack of moral fibre. Two solutions to the problem were legislative restrictions on emigration and a "call for national unity," including the return of emigrant Swedes. In 1907 representatives of this faction introduced a motion in the Swedish Parliament for the creation of a "national labor exchange office to serve the interests of Swedish residents abroad." Herman Lagercrantz, appointed Swedish minister to Washington that same year, expressed the hope that no energy would be spared in turning the tide of emigration. It was even suggested that Crown Prince Gustav (later King Gustav V) be sent as a goodwill ambassador to the Swedish settlements to drum up support for remigration. This coalition of conservatives and ultranationalists also founded the National Association Against Emigration *(Nationalföreningen mot emigrationen)* in 1907 for the purpose of checking the spread of America fever and encouraging the repatriation of Sweden's prodigal sons and daughters. Aside from distributing antiemigration literature, the association lent its support to the Private Home Ownership Movement *(Eg-nahemsrörelsen)*, which worked for the improvement of living conditions among Swedish workers and the redevelopment of districts in northern Sweden.

According to liberal reformist circles, however, there was another side to the emigration issue. While recognizing the blood-letting effects on population growth, they called attention to the symptoms in Swedish society responsible for the exodus. The primary goal was to isolate the causes of emigration and solve them with social reforms, and it was this thinking that lay behind the creation of the National Commission on Emigration *(Emigrationsutredningen)* by the Swedish Parliament in 1907. Chosen to head the commission was a rather eccentric statistician by the name of Gustaf Sundbärg. Over the next six years the commission investigated emigration from every possible angle, including immigrant conditions in America. Its final report, complete with twenty appendixes, was published in 1913. The report outlined the reforms necessary to curb emigration. The major thrust of the commission's findings was highlighted by Sundbärg himself in his concluding statement: "The most effective means of halting emigration rests with us as a society. If we are to be prepared to meet the future it is imperative that we progress socially as well as economically."[2] Specific reforms in the commission's report included the redistribution of farmland, the stimulation of industrial expansion, the promotion of the Private Home Ownership Movement, the extension of compulsory public education, and the passage of liberal voting-rights legislation.

In the final analysis, the thinking of the emigration commission and liberal political circles set the tone for Sweden's constructive reaction to the emigration issue. While it is difficult to credit either side with the passage of specific reforms, it can be said that emigration opened the eyes of the Swedish government to the need for industrial development and the imperative of social reform.

Economic and Political Consequences

Opponents of emigration frequently argued that the exodus of young, able-bodied Swedes was robbing the country of its labor potential and undermining its tax basis. The loss to the nation was a staggering one, and they claimed they had the figures to prove it—right down to the last emigrant.

Today the perspective is altogether different, and most Swedish historians credit emigration with having functioned as a safety valve for an overpopulated and underdeveloped country. In effect, emigration gave Swedish society a chance to breathe and spared it from a wave of radical transitions in the march from a predominantly agricultural to an industrial economy. Even more positive were the contributions of emigrants to the flow of American goods and capital across the Atlantic. The production of cheap foodstuffs, such as American wheat and meat, found a ready market in Sweden and stimulated the process of industrialization. At the same time the influx of American dollars stabilized the Swedish economy. It is estimated that Swedish emigrants sent home 8 million dollars each year during the period 1906 to 1930. For the 1920s alone, this figure represented 7.5 percent of the annual profits in the Swedish lumber industry, or 2 percent of the annual profits in Swedish agriculture, or 25 percent of Sweden's balance of payments aboard. Returning emigrants and visiting Yankees proved a stimulating source of new ideas for Swedish industry, especially the export branch which was anxious to accommodate the latest marketing trends around the turn of the century. In fact, ten of the men behind the breakthrough of rolling mills in the Swedish iron industry had originally emigrated to America.

On the surface, at least, emigration would seem to have had a sizeable impact on Swedish politics, precisely because it coincided with the rise of the Swedish working-class movement. Actually, the influence was minimal. The Social-Democratic ideals of the Swedish labor movement were completely different from the spirit of rugged individualism that flourished on the

American frontier. As far as Swedish workers were concerned, the emigrants had clearer sympathies with the old order of things. Their America letters and return visits paid constant homage to the free-enterprise system, while their vision of a true democracy seemed to be a simple matter of "equal opportunity for all comers." On the whole, Swedish Americans have not had the reputation of being warm to the idea of socialism or organized labor. All of these elements, then, reinforce the picture of the Swedish emigrant as a remote and passive bystander to the political struggle of the Swedish working class.

On the other hand, emigration did have an impact on the movement for social reform in Sweden. It dramatized the cause of left-wing political circles and inspired the thinking of the emigration commission in its recommendations for liberalized voting reforms. While reformers were well aware of the faults in Swedish society and often looked to America for fresh insights, they used a critical eye in sorting out the problems and their solutions. In sum, the interplay of push and pull factors that shaped the course of Swedish emigration also had a hand in reshaping the contours of Swedish society.

Emigration in Swedish Literature

It is only recently that emigration has won a place for itself in Sweden's national literature. Much of the credit lies with the gifted pen of Vilhelm Moberg, whose documentary novels on the early Småland emigrants captured the imagination of readers on both sides of the Atlantic. There were others before Moberg, however, who wrote from their own emigrant experiences or took their themes from emigrant settings in both countries.

The peak years of Swedish emigration inspired a flurry of popular commemorative poems in the columns of Swedish newspapers. Nearly all of them were tendentious: they either applauded the emigrants for their defiant departure from an ingracious society or denounced their treacherous betrayal of a loving Mother Sweden. One anonymous poem entitled "En svensk emigrants avskedsord" (The Parting Words of a Swedish

Emigrant), originally published in *Hvad Nytt* in April, 1869, illustrates the positive side of the picture.

Jag reser åt Amerika, farväl du gamla Norden.
Jag frusit nog och slitit ont, för kär i fosterjorden.
Men drivorna på tuvorna
samt klipporna med sipporna
jag lämnar åt poeterna,
som leva blott av orden.

Men den som fått, likt mig, en kropp och uti kroppen mage,
han slite alla fördomsband och över havet drage.
Men där kan bli en fågel fri.
Här slavar vi, nu arma bi,
och draga honung endast i
de vise som regera.

. . . .

Vi trogna bi dra't honung nog åt alla feta drönar,
Vi lämna er i frid och ro, tillika alla björnar.
Som suget all den must vi skänkt.
Nu har ni oss på flykten skrämt,
men fri står världens dörr på glänt.
Dit vi nu alla strömma.

I'm bound for young America,
Farewell old Scandinavia.
I've had my fill of cold and toil,
All for the love of mother soil.
You poets with your rocks and rills
Can stay to starve—on words, no frills.

Me, I've got a stomach 'neath my hide,
No bonds can keep me on this side.
There, out west, a man breathes free,
While here one slaves, a tired bee,
Gathering honey to fill the hive
Of wise old rulers, on us they thrive.

. . . .

In toil we hover before their thrones,
While they take to slumber, like lazy drones.
Drunk with our nectar they've set us afright,
But opportunity has knocked, and we'll take our flight.[3]

The negative side can be represented by a few verses from a more literary work, "Frivillig landsflykt" (Voluntary Exile), written by an associate professor at the University of Uppsala, C. L. Östergren, under the pen name of Fjalar:

Skam åt den som fanan sviker,
skam åt den som fegsint viker
undan stridens nöd och fara
för att vinna veklig ro!
Mod, och hindren undanträngas!
Mod och alla klippor sprängas!
Är din jord än karg, kan lyckan
blomma rikt i torftigt bo.

Tvekar än du otacksamme?
Så välan vid målet framme,
skall du fåfängt åter tråna
till det hem du flyktat från.
Hör du? Vredgad nordan tjuter,
med förakt var bölja skjuter
bort från fosterjordens stränder
trolös, pliktförgäten son.

Shame on those who their flag would spurn,
Shame on those who so cowardly turn
From the din of battle and the call to arms
To seek their peace in elusive charms!
Courage my friend, and your hopes will prevail!
Courage my friend, and all mountains you scale!
Though meagre your land, success is your lot,
If in poverty you bear the fruit of your plot.

Hesitate you still, cold ungrateful soul?
Though close you be now to your chosen goal,
You would vainly regain the land of your heart,
From whence you did yearn and took your depart?
Hear, how the north winds rage with one might,
Hear, how the ocean's waves sweep at one sight
The likes of you, faithless prodigal son,
From the shores of this land, whose love you had won![4]

It was only a matter of time before some of Sweden's leading lyricists whetted their own poetic appetites on the emigrant gristmill. There was a natural fascination with the making of a Swedish America and the shaping of an immigrant personality, although some writers turned this into an open invitation for stereotyping. In a real sense, the emigration era opened for the broad masses of Swedish society their first major contacts with another culture. Up to that time the spread of cultural impulses from such countries as England and France had catered only to the upper classes. America's influence, on the other hand, was rooted in the emigrants themselves, who represented the grass roots of Swedish society. The reaction of the cultural elite to this new influence was negative, even scornful, and the writers who curried its favors followed suit. In their eyes, the returning Swedish American symbolized the inflated optimism of simple-minded souls whose only dream was to emigrate to America. While it would be unfair to call Gustaf Fröding a tendentious poet in this respect, some of this thinking flavors his immensely popular poem "Farväll" (Farewell), written in 1890. The following verses are meant to describe the feelings of one Swedish immigrant, who fell victim to unrequited love and was forced to make the journey alone.

> Tre dollars haver jag om dagen
> och är en herrkar efter lagen
> Du kunde varit mistriss nu,
> men den som slapp te bli't, va du.

> Du kunde gått i hatt och handsker
> ibland tjangtile amerkansker
> och lefft på gås och rebbenspjäll,
> men faderväll, men faderväll!

> Three dollars I pocket from work, morn to night.
> A gentleman's title is my full legal right.
> Had you but followed, you'd be a miss with a dress,
> But you were the one who wouldn't say yes.

A hat and kid gloves could have marked your appeal
Among American folk, whose ways are "genteel."
On wild goose and pork ribs a lifetime you'd dwell,
But goodbye to all that, farewell, fare thee well.[5]

The Free Churches and the Temperance Movement

It is not surprising that the Swedish free churches took an active role in spreading America's cultural influence throughout Sweden. Their own organizational history owed much to the missionary zeal of American churches. Mormon and Baptist preachers reached Sweden as early as the 1850s and 1860s. A decade later American Methodists built upon earlier influences in winning new territory for Swedish Methodism. The Pentecostal movement came much later, during the decade before World War I, but even it was inspired from America.

There were two stages in the history of the Swedish temperance movement. The first evolved during the early 1800s under the leadership of Peter Wieselgren, a Lutheran clergyman and outspoken temperance supporter. The second, an Anglo-American creation, came at the end of the 1870s and went much farther than its predecessor in advocating a program of total abstinence. The first Swedish lodge of the International Order of Good Templars (IOGT) was established in 1879 by a former Swedish emigrant, Olov Bergström. In 1884 the Good Templar Order *(Templarorden)* was launched as an exclusively Swedish-American product. Two years later the Swedish Blue Ribbon movement *(Blåbands-föreningen)* arrived on the scene and followed the American pattern of combining temperance reform with religious revival.

All of these developments, then, enhanced the impact of American culture on Swedish society and underlined the broader implications of the emigration process. Sweden's progressive assimilation of American culture since the early 1900s, however, is an entirely different story and has hardly anything to do with emigration or Swedish America.

Remigration

Remigration to Europe was strongest among the new immigrant waves from southern and eastern Europe, particularly the Italians and Greeks. Part of the explanation lies in the fact that most of them settled in urban areas and did not establish ties to farms and homesteads. Of even greater significance, however, were the underlying motives of the emigrants and the nature of their stay in America. Large numbers of them came in search of temporary work which would pay their journey home and enable them to invest the rest of their earnings in a farm or business.

Due to the rural and family-oriented character of early Swedish emigration there was little remigration to Sweden up until the 1880s. After that the pattern changed, and the steady influx of working-class immigrants to American industries and urban centers accelerated the pace of remigration during the 1900s. Although it cannot be compared with the trend among southern European immigrants, Swedish remigration stabilized at a relatively high level and finally surpassed emigration during the 1930s, when conditions improved in Sweden. The first regular statistics on Swedish remigration date from 1875. From that year up to 1930 around 175,000 persons, or roughly 18 percent of the emigrants during that period, returned home.

Who were they, and why did they return? Basically, there were two categories of remigrants. The first had never planned to stay in America for any length of time, but simply used the move as a means of finding temporary but well-paying jobs. Most of them intended to invest their earnings in a farm back home, and this determined their objectives on the American labor market. American industry was crying for manpower, and there were good wages to be made in lumber camps and in building railroads. Emigrants from Småland and Dalsland seized on these opportunities with particular enthusiasm and turned them to their own advantage. Confirmation of this comes from Långasjö parish, located in the "emigration belt" of Kronobergs *län*, where roughly one-third of the farms were bought with the savings of former emigrants.

The second category of remigrants was dramatically different from the first, both in terms of prospects and end results. Statistics show that they left America almost as soon as they arrived. Obviously, something had gone wrong with the American experiment: the adjustment to a new language, a new society, and a new labor market placed far more demands on them than they had expected or were able to meet. Under the circumstances, then, remigration loomed as the lesser of two evils.

Whatever the motives for remigration, the timing was generally the same. Peak years of emigration were always followed by a surge of remigration, and the American economic picture weighed heavily in the balance. The recessions and panics of 1884, 1893, 1903, and 1907 had a levelling effect on immigrant labor and generated major waves of remigration. In 1894, for example, remigration accounted for 77 percent of the year's new arrivals. A breakdown of remigration by occupational groups shows that Swedish-American farmers were least affected by these developments. Higher up on the scale came the ranks of industrial labor, while the primary targets were white-collar workers, skilled technicians, college and university graduates, as well as business and professional people. That urban wage-earners had a greater tendency to remigrate than self-sufficient farmers is not surprising, especially when one considers their overall mobility in American society.

The greatest tide of Swedish remigration was felt in farming districts, where former emigrants tended to settle in their old parishes. Despite their contacts with the American urban environment, the majority chose not to become city dwellers after their return to Sweden. Remigration was particularly weak to sections of northern Sweden due to a high level of family emigration past the turn of the century and the decline of the sawmill industry after 1890. A final characteristic of Swedish remigration was its one-sided sexual distribution: over two-thirds of the remigrants were men.

Remigration to Sweden usually meant a return to old and

familiar environments, both geographically and socially. While there were always those who put their American dollars to work, bought their own farms, or paid off old debts, the vast majority settled for less, including a modest improvement in their social status. The following comments made by a clergyman to the Swedish emigration commission in 1908 illustrate what this meant, "Many homeowners in Hishults parish are former emigrants. The greatest material and spiritual blessings they have afforded the community are their efficiency, their energy, and their own wealth of experience. Equally important are the small savings they have managed to bring back, which enable them to work their farms in a more up-to-date fashion."[6]

In most cases, then, the journey home was a return to ordinary, everyday living but with the added seasoning of a few insightful years as an immigrant on another shore. Over a million Swedes never returned, however, and it was their dreams and labors that helped to shape the American nation.

Census Table

Notes

Selected Bibliography

Census Table
Emigration and Remigration, 1851–1971

Year	Emigration	Remigration
1851	931	——
1861	758	——
1871	12,985	——
1881	40,620	553
1891	36,143	3,546
1901	20,306	3,621
1911	15,571	4,411
1921	5,430	4,387
1931	919	4,810
1941	289	262
1951	2,662	1,340
1961	1,727	1,699
1971	1,592	1,860

Statistics taken from Official Reports of the Swedish Commission on Emigration *(Emigrationsutredningen),* supplement to Sweden's Official Statistics *(Bidrag till Sveriges off. stat.):* Population 1900–1910, Emigration and Remigration 1911–38, and Statistical Yearbook *(Statistisk årsbok)* 1945, 1950, 1955, 1965, 1970, 1975. For a much more complete set of census tables and information see the original Swedish version, *Den stora utvandringen.*

Notes

1. They Left for America

1. *Öresunds Posten* (Helsingborg), April 19, 1869.
2. George M. Stephenson, ed. and trans., "Typical America Letters," in the Swedish Historical Society *Yearbook* 7 (1921–22), 54–55. Also cited in H. Arnold Barton, *Letters from the Promised Land. Swedes in America, 1840–1914* (Minneapolis: University of Minnesota Press, 1975), p. 87.
3. George M. Stephenson, ed. and trans., "*Hemlandet* Letters," in the Swedish Historical Society *Yearbook* 8 (1922–23), 127–28. Also in Barton, p. 117.
4. Stephenson, "Typical America Letters," p. 71, and Barton, p. 98.
5. Stephenson, "Typical America Letters," p. 77, and Barton, p. 101.
6. *Emigrationsutredningen* [Swedish Commission on Emigration], *Bilaga* II [Supplement II] (Stockholm, 1909), p. 154. Translated in Barton, pp. 265–66.
7. *Report on the Population of the United States at the Eleventh Census 1890* (Washington, DC, 1895), I, xxxiv.

2. Group Emigration from Sweden

1. Fredrika Bremer, *Hemmen i den nya verlden* (Stockholm: P.A. Norstedt, 1853), II, 258–59. Translated here by Kermit B. Westerberg.
2. George M. Stephenson, "Documents Relating to Peter Cassel and the Settlement at New Sweden," in *Swedish American Historical Society Bulletin*, vol. 2, no. 1 (1929), 55–62. Also in H. Arnold Barton, *Letters from the Promised Land*, pp. 28–33.
3. Albin Widén, *När Svensk-Amerika grundades. Emigrantbrev med kommentarer* [When Swedish America Was Founded. Emigrant Letters with Commentaries], (Stockholm: Vasa Orden av Amerika, 1961), p. 20.

4. Hans Mattson, *Reminiscences. The Story of an Emigrant* (St. Paul: D. D. Merrill Company, 1892), p. 52.

3. Mass Emigration from Sweden

1. *Emigrationsutredningen, Bilaga* VII (Stockholm, 1908), p. 238.
2. Ibid.
3. Ibid., p. 169.
4. Karl August Modén, *Wilhelm Lindblom. En levnadsteckning* [Wilhelm Lindblom. A Biography], (Stockholm: B.-M.:s Förlag, 1929), p. 177.
5. Regarding "Petter Jönssons resa till Amerika" see p. 36. An English version of the ballad can be found in Robert L. Wright, *Swedish Emigrant Ballads* (Lincoln, NE: University of Nebraska Press, 1965), pp. 108–9.
6. *Emigrationsutredningen, Bilaga* VII, p. 144. Translated in H. Arnold Barton, p. 13.
7. *Emigrationsutredningen, Bilaga* XVII (Stockholm, 1919), p. 119.
8. *Emigrationsutredningen, Bilaga* VII (Stockholm, 1908), p. 258.
9. Ibid., p. 254.
10. Ibid., pp. 252, 259.
11. Ibid., *Bilaga* II (Stockholm, 1908), p. 86.
12. Interview by Lennart Setterdahl for *Emigrantinstitutet,* Växjö, Sweden. Published in Fritjof Bengtsson, ed., *Halländska emigrantöden 1860—1930* (The Fortunes of Halland Emigrants, 1860—1930), Halmstad: Hallands Bildningsförbund/Bokförlaget Spektra AB, 1976).
13. *Emigrationsutredningen, Betänkande* (Stockholm, 1913), p. 872.
14. Ibid., *Bilaga* VIII (Stockholm, 1910), p. 62.
15. Ibid., *Bilaga* VII (Stockholm, 1908), p. 246.

5. They Sold America

1. C. A. Perkins, Stockholm, to State Department, Washington, DC, Despatch No. 24 (November 24, 1868), Department of State Papers, National Archives, Washington, DC
2. State Department to C. C. Andrews, March 13, 1871. U.S. Legation in Stockholm, Department of State Papers, National Archives, Washington, DC.
3. Carl Roos, "Vasa, Goodhue County, Minnesota. Dess Förste Settlare," [Vasa, Goodhue County, Minnesota. The First Settlers], *Minnesota Stats Tidning,* February 1, 1877. This article has been translated in the *Yearbook* of the Swedish Historical Society of America, 10 (1924–25): 88–113; excerpt from p. 104 of the article retranslated by Kermit B. Westerberg.
4. *Emigrationsutredningen, Bilaga* VII, p. 175.
5. George M. Stephenson, "*Hemlandet* Letters," in the Swedish Historical Society of America *Yearbook* 8 (1922–23), 152. Also in H. Arnold Barton, *Letters from the Promised Land,* p. 141.

6. Bound for America

1. George M. Stephenson, ed. and trans., "Typical American Letters," in the Swedish Historical Society *Yearbook* 7 (1921–22), 93–95. The translation used here has been supplied by Kermit B. Westerberg.
2. *Hemlandet* (Chicago), May 5, 1868.
3. E. Gustav Johnson, ed. and trans., "An Immigrant's Letter of 1869," *Swedish Pioneer Historical Quarterly*, vol. 9, no. 1 (January 1960), 21–25.
4. Letter from Hans Mattson to Mrs. Mattson, dated January 27, 1869. Hans Mattson Papers, Manuscript Department, Minnesota Historical Society, St. Paul, MN.
5. *Emigrationsutredningen, Bilaga* VII, p. 138.
6. Ibid., p. 174.
7. Fritjof Bengtsson, ed., *Halländska emigrantöden*, p. 215.

7. Who Were They and Where Did They Settle?

1. This section is based on Otto R. Landelius's manuscript on Swedish place-names in the United States. Landelius's imposing research findings are planned for publication by the Swedish Pioneer Historical Society, Chicago.

8. Swedes Become Americans

1. *Hemlandet* (Chicago), September 16, 1861. Reprinted in Hans Mattson, *Reminiscences. The Story of an Emigrant* (St. Paul: D. D. Merill 1892), p. 60.
2. "Steam From the Melting Pot. There is a Replica of Explosive Europe on U.S. Ground. Can We Transform it into a Working Model of Political Warfare?," *Fortune*, vol. 26, no. 3 (September 1942), 76.
3. Swedish version printed in Nils Hasselmo, *Amerikasvenska* (Lund: Esselte Studium, 1974), p. 32; English translation by Kermit B. Westerberg.
4. Ibid., p. 33; translation by Kermit B. Westerberg.
5. Undated manscript in Hans Mattson Papers, Manuscript Department, Minnesota Historical Society, St. Paul, MN.

9. Americanization

1. Fritjof Bengtsson, Ed., *Halländska emigrantöden*, p. 128.

10. The Consequences of Emigration in Sweden

1. C. C. Andrews to State Department, Despatch No. 93 (March 3, 1871), U. S. Legation in Stockholm, Department of State Papers, National Archives, Washington, D. C.

2. *Emigrationsutredningen, Betänkande* (Stockholm, 1913), p. 890.

3. English translation by Kermit B. Westerberg.

4. Carl Ludvig Östergren, *Nya Dikter* [New Poems], (Stockholm: Norstedt, 1879), pp. 106–7. English translation by Kermit B. Westerberg.

5. Gustaf Fröding, *Gitarr och dragharmonika* [Guitar and Hand-clavier], (Stockholm: Albert Bonnier, 1891), p. 48. English translation by Kermit B. Westerberg.

6. *Emigrationsutredningen, Bilaga* XVII (Stockholm, 1909), p. 161.

Selected Bibliography

The first two sections of this bibliography list works of a general and introductory nature on the topic of Swedish emigration to America, while the third section is devoted to more specialized literature that has reference to specific chapters in this book. Those interested in studying a particular aspect of Swedish emigration will find this literature helpful as a guide to additional titles in both English and Swedish. Although this bibliography concentrates on English-language titles as a matter of principle, it does include references to a number of central works in Swedish.

Bibliographies

Ander, O. Fritiof. *The Cultural Heritage of the Swedish Immigrant: Selected References.* Augustana Library Publications, no. 27.

Larson, Esther Elisabeth. *Swedish Commentators on America, 1638–1865: An Annotated List of Selected Manuscript and Printed Materials.* New York and Chicago: The New York Public Library and the Swedish Pioneer Historical Society, 1963.

General Reading

Babcock, Kendric C. *The Scandinavian Element in the United States.* Urbana, IL: University of Illinois, 1914.

Beijbom, Ulf. *Amerika! Amerika! En bok om utvandringen* [America! America! A Book About the Emigration]. Stockholm: Natur och Kultur, 1977.

Benson, Adolph B., and Hedin, Naboth. *Americans from Sweden.* Philadelphia: J. B. Lippincott, 1950.

Emigrationsutredningen. Betänkande och bilagor [The Swedish Commission on Emigration. Report and Supplements]. 20 vols. Stockholm: n.p., 1908–1913.

Fleicher, Eric W. and Weibull, Jörgen. *Viking Times to Modern: The Story of Swedish Exploring and Settlement in America and the Development of Trade and Shipping from the Vikings to Our Time.* Stockholm and Minneapolis: University of Minnesota Press, 1954.

Friis, Erik, ed. *The Scandinavian Presence in North America.* New York: Harper's Magazine Press, 1976.

Hasselmo, Nils, ed. *Perspectives on Swedish Immigration. Proceedings of the International Conference on the Swedish Heritage in the Upper Midwest, April 1–3, 1976, University of Minnesota, Duluth.* Chicago and Duluth: Swedish Pioneer Historical Society and University of Minnesota, Duluth, 1978.

Kastrup, Allen. *The Swedish Heritage in America: The Swedish Element in America and American-Swedish Relations in Their Historical Perspective.* Minneapolis: Swedish Council of America, 1975.

Koblik, Steven, ed. *Sweden's Development from Poverty to Affluence, 1750–1970.* Minneapolis: University of Minnesota Press, 1975.

Lindberg, John S. *The Background of Swedish Emigration to the United Statees: An Economic and Sociological Study in the Dynamics of Migration.* Minneapolis: University of Minnesota Press, 1930.

Nelson, Helge. *The Swedes and the Swedish Settlements in North America* (Studier utgivna av Kungliga Humanistiska Vetenskapssamfundet i Lund. 38.) 2 vols. Lund: CWK Gleerup, 1943.

Nyblom, Gösta, ed. *Americans of Swedish Descent.* Rock Island, IL: G. Nyblom Publishing House, 1948.

Runblom, Harald and Norman, Hans, eds. *From Sweden to America: A History of the Migration. A Collective Work of the Uppsala Migration Research Project.* Minneapolis and Uppsala: University of Minnesota Press and Acta Universitatis Upsaliensis, University of Uppsala, 1976.

Scott, Franklin D. *Sweden: The Nation's History.* Minneapolis: University of Minnesota Press, 1977.

Skarstedt, Ernst T. *Svensk-amerikanska folket i helg och söcken* [The Swedish-American People at Work and at Leisure]. Stockholm: Björck and Börjesson, 1917.

Stephenson, George M. *A History of American Immigration 1820–1924.* Boston: Ginn and Company, 1926.

Westman, Erik G. and Johnson, E. Gustav, eds. *The Swedish Element in America.* 4 vols. Chicago: Swedish-American Biographical Society, 1931 and 1934.

Wittke, Carl F. *We Who Built America: The Saga of the Immigrant.* Cleveland: Press of Western Reserve University, 1964.

Attention can also be drawn to articles in the *Swedish Pioneer Historical Quarterly (SPHQ),* a publication of the Swedish Pioneer Historical Society in Chicago,

Illinois. Since its first issue in 1950, the *Quarterly* has covered nearly every aspect of Swedish emigration and Swedish-American life and also enabled Swedish historians to present some of their research findings to the American public.

Specific Readings

Åkerman, Sune; Kronborg, Bo; and Nilsson, Thomas. "Emigration, Family and Kinship." *Nordic Population Mobility. American Studies in Scandinavia,* 9, Nos. 1–2 (1977), 105–22.

Ander, O. Fritiof. "Public Officials." In *Swedes in America, 1638–1938,* pp. 321–37. Edited by Adolph Benson and Naboth Hedin. New Haven, CT: Yale University Press, 1938.

——————. *T. N. Hasselquist. The Career and Influence of a Swedish-American Clergyman, Journalist and Educator.* Rock Island, IL: Augustana Library Publications, 1931.

Andersson, Theodore. *100 Years. A History of Bishop Hill.* Chicago: Theodore Anderson, 1946.

Arden, G. Everett. *Augustana Heritage. A History of the Augustana Lutheran Church.* Rock Island, Il.: Augustana College, 1962.

Aronson, Johan Hugo, and Brockman, L. O. *The Galloping Swede.* Missoula, MT: Mountain Press Publishing, 1970.

Backlund, Oscar J. *A Century of the Swedish American Press.* Chicago: Swedish American Newspaper Company, 1952.

Barton, H. Arnold. "Clio and Swedish America: Historians, Organizations, Publications." In *Perspectives on Swedish Immigration,* pp. 3–24. Edited by Nils Hasselmo. Chicago and Duluth: Swedish Pioneer Historical Society and University of Minnesota, Duluth, 1978.

Beijbom, Ulf. *Swedes in Chicago. A Demographic and Social Study of the 1846–1880 Immigration.* Studia Historica Upsaliensia, no. 38. Stockholm: Scandinavian University Books, 1971.

Bergendoff, Conrad. *Augustana . . . A Profession of Faith: A History of Augustana College, 1860–1936,* Rock Island, IL: Augustana College Library, 1969.

——————. "The Role of Augustana in the Transplanting of a Culture Across the Atlantic." In *The Immigration of Ideas: Studies in the North Atlantic Community.* Essays presented to Fritiof Ander, pp. 67–83. Rock Island, IL: Augustana Historical Society, 1968.

Bonsor, Noel R. P. *North Atlantic Seaway. An Illustrated History of the Passenger Service Linking the Old World and the New.* Prescot, Lancashire: T. Stephenson, 1955.

Brattne, Berit, in cooperation with Åkerman, Sune. "The Importance of the Transport Sector for Mass Emigration." In *From Sweden to America,* pp. 176–200. Edited by Harald Runblom and Hans Norman. Minneapolis and Uppsala: University of Minnesota Press and University of Uppsala, 1976.

Capps, Finis Herbert. *From Isolationism to Involvement: The Swedish Immigrant Press in America, 1914–1943.* Chicago: Swedish Pioneer Historical Society, 1966.

Carlsson, Sten. "Chronology and Composition of Swedish Emigration to America." In *From Sweden to America,* pp. 114–48. Edited by Harald Runblom and Hans Norman. Minneapolis and Uppsala: University of Minnesota Press and University of Uppsala, 1976.

—————. "Scandinavian Politicians in Minnesota Around the Turn of the Century. A Study in the Role of the Ethnic Factor in an Immigrant State." In *Americana Norvegica.* Studies in Scandinavian-American Interrelations Dedicated to Einar Haugen, vol. 3, 237–71. Oslo: Universitets Forlaget, 1971.

—————. "Swedes in Politics." In *From Sweden to America,* pp. 291–300. Edited by Harald Runbolm and Hans Norman. Minneapolis and Uppsala: University of Minnesota Press and University of Uppsala, 1976.

Davidsson, Rune. "Den tidiga emigrationen från Kisa socken 1845–1860" [The Early Emigration from Kisa Parish 1845–1860]. In *Svensk 1800-tals emigration* Meddelanden från Historiska institutionen i Göteborg, no. 1, pp. 15–42. Gothenburg: Historiska institutionen, Göteborgs universitet, 1969.

Eidevall, Gunnar. *Vilhelm Mobergs emigrantepos* [Vilhelm Moberg's Emigrant Epic]. Stockholm: Norstedt, 1974.

Elmen, Paul. *Wheat Flour Messiah: Eric Jansson of Bishop Hill.* Carbondale, IL: Southern Illinois University Press and Swedish Pioneer Historical Society, 1976.

Erickson, Charlotte. *American Industry and the European Immigrant, 1860–1888.* Cambridge, MA: Harvard University Press, 1957.

Espelie, E. M., and Dowie, J. I., eds. *The Swedish Immigrant Community in Transition. Essays in Honor of Dr. Conrad Bergendoff.* Augustana Historical Society Publication no. 20. Rock Island, IL: Augustana Historical Society, 1963.

Gates, Paul Wallace. *The Illinois Central Railroad and Its Colonization Work.* Cambridge, MA: Harvard University Press, 1934.

Gibbs, Charles Robert Vernon. *British Passenger Lines of the Five Oceans.* London: Putnam, 1963.

Hasselmo, Nils. *Amerikasvenska. En bok om språkutvecklingen i Svensk-Amerika* [American Swedish. A Book about the Linguistic Development in Swedish America] Skrifter utgivna av Svenska språknämnden, no. 51. Lund: Esselte Studium, 1874.

—————. "The Language Question." In *Perspectives on Swedish Immigration,* pp. 225–43. Edited by Nils Hasselmo. Chicago and Duluth: Swedish Pioneer Historical Society and University of Minnesota, Duluth, 1978.

Hansen, Marcus L. *The Atlantic Migration 1607–1860.* New York: Harper, 1961.

Helmes, Winifred. *John A. Johnson, the People's Governor: A Political Biography.* Minneapolis: University of Minnesota Press, 1949.

Hokanson, Nels. *Swedish Immigrants in Lincoln's Time.* New York: Harper and Brothers, 1942.

Isaksson, Olov, and Hallgren, Sören. *Bishop Hill: A Utopia on the Prairie.* Stockholm: L T:s Förlag, 1969.

Johansson, Sven G. *Historical Review of the Vasa Order of America, 1896–1971.* N. p.: Vasa Order of America, 1974.

Johnson, Amandus. *The Swedish Settlements on the Delaware, 1638–1664.* 2 vols. Philadelphia: University of Pennsylvania, 1911.

Johnson, E. Gustav. "A Selected Bibliography of Bishop Hill Literature." *Swedish Pioneer Historical Quarterly (SPHQ)* 15, No. 3 (July 1964), 109–22.

Johnson, Emeroy. *Eric Norelius: Pioneer Midwest Pastor and Churchman.* Rock Island, IL: Augustana Book Concern, 1954.

Kälvemark, Ann-Sofie. "Fear of Military Service—A Cause of Emigration?" In *From Sweden to America,* pp. 164–75. Edited by Harald Runbolm and Hans Norman. Minneapolis and Uppsala: University of Minnesota Press and University of Uppsala, 1976.

————. "Swedish Emigration Policy in an International Perspective, 1840–1925." In *From Sweden to America,* pp. 94–113. Edited by Harald Runbolm and Hans Norman. Minneapolis and Uppsala: University of Minnesota Press and University of Uppsala, 1976.

Kaups, Matti. "Swedish Immigrants in Duluth, 1856–1870." In *Perspectives on Swedish Immigration,* pp. 166–98. Edited by Nils Hasselmo. Chicago and Duluth: Swedish Pioneer Historical Society and University of Minnesota, Duluth, 1978.

Larson, Bruce L. *Lindbergh of Minnesota: A Political Biography.* New York: Harcourt Brace Jovanovich, 1973.

————. "Swedish Americans and Farmer-Labor Politics in Minnesota." In *Perspectives on Swedish Immigration,* pp. 206–24. Edited by Nils Hasselmo. Chicago and Duluth: Swedish Pioneer Historical Society and University of Minnesota, Duluth, 1978.

Lext, Gösta. *Studier rörande svensk emigration till Nordamerika 1850–1880: registrering, propaganda, agenter, transporter och resvägar* [Studies on Swedish Emigration to North America, 1850–1880. Registration, Propaganda, Agents, Transports and Travel Routes] Gothenburg: Göteborgs Landsarkiv, 1977.

Lindmark, Sture. *Swedish America, 1914–1932: Studies in Ethnicity with Emphasis on Illinois and Minnesota.* Studia Historica Upsaliensis, no. 37. Stockholm and Chicago: Scandinavian University Books and Swedish Pioneer Historical Society, 1971.

Lindquist, Emory. *An Immigrant's American Odyssey: A Biography of Ernst Skarstedt.* Rock Island, IL: Augustana Historical Society, 1974.

——. *Bethany in Kansas: The History of a College.* Lindsborg, KA: Bethany College, 1975.

——. "The Swedish-Born Population and the Swedish Stock: The United States Census of 1960 and Comparative Data with Some Concluding Observations." *SPHQ,* 16, No. 2 (April 1965), 76–90.

——. *Vision of a Valley: Olof Olsson and the Early History of Lindsborg.* Rock Island, IL: Augustana Historical Society, 1970.

Ljungmark, Lars. *For Sale—Minnesota: Organized Promotion of Scandinavian Immigration 1886–1873.* Studia Historica Gothoburgensia, no. 13. Chicago and Gothenburg: Swedish Pioneer Historical Society and Scandinavian University Books, 1973.

——. "General C. C. Andrews, High-Placed Immigration Agent in Sweden." *SPHQ,* 21, No. 2 (April 1970), 84–104.

——. "Hans Mattson's Reminiscences—A Swedish-American Monument." *SPHQ,* 29, No. 1 (January 1978), 57–68.

——. "Notes from a Travel Diary." *SPHQ,* 11, No. 3 (July 1960), 108–15.

Lonn, Ella. *Foreigners in the Confederacy.* Chapel Hill, NC: University of North Carolina Press, 1940.

——. *Foreigners in the Union Army and Navy.* Baton Rouge: Louisiana State University Press, 1951.

Lucas, Richard. *Charles August Lindbergh, Sr. A Case Study of Congressional Insurgency, 1906–1912.* Studia Historica Upsaliensia, no. 61. Uppsala: Acta Universitatis Upsaliensis, 1974.

Mattson, Hans. *Reminiscences: The Story of an Emigrant.* St. Paul: D. D. Merrill Company, 1892.

Mayer, George H. *The Political Career of Floyd B. Olsson.* Minneapolis: University of Minnesota Press, 1951.

Nordstrom, Byron, ed. *The Swedes in Minnesota.* Minneapolis: T. S. Denison, 1976.

——. "The Sixth Ward: a Minneapolis Swede Town in 1905." In *Perspectives on Swedish Immigration,* pp. 151–65. Edited by Nils Hasselmo. Chicago and Duluth: Swedish Pioneer Historical Society and University of Minnesota, Duluth, 1978.

Norelius, Eric. *De Svenska Lutherska Församlingarnas och Svenskarnas Historia i Amerika* [History of the Swedes and the Swedish Lutheran Congregations in America] 2 vols. Rock Island, IL: Lutheran Augustana Book Concern, 1916.

Norman, Hans. *Från Bergslagen till Nordamerika. Studier i migrationsmönster, social rörlighet och demografisk struktur med utgångspunkt från Örebro län 1851–1915* [From Bergslagen to North America. Studies in Migration Pattern, Social Mobility and Demographic Structure on the Basis of Örebro *län*, 1851–1915]. Studia Historica Upsaliensia, no. 62. Uppsala: Acta Universitatis Upsaliensis, 1974.

————. "Causes of Emigration: An Attempt at a Multivariate Analysis." In *From Sweden to America*, pp. 149–63. Edited by Harald Runblom and Hans Norman. Minneapolis and Uppsala: University of Minnesota Press and University of Uppsala, 1976.

————. "Swedes in North America." In *From Sweden to America*, pp. 228–90. Edited by Harald Runblom and Hans Norman. Minneapolis and Uppsala: University of Minnesota Press and University of Uppsala, 1976.

Nyberg, Janet. "Swedish Language Newspapers in Minnesota." In *Prespectives on Swedish Immigration*, pp. 244–55. Edited by Nils Hasselmo. Chicago and Duluth: Swedish Pioneer Historical Society and University of Minnesota, Duluth, 1978.

Nystrom, Daniel. *A Ministry of Printing: A History of the Publication House of the Augustana Lutheran Church*. Rock Island, IL: Augustana Press, 1962.

Öberg, Kjell, reporting commissioner. *Utvandrarnas tidningar. Betänkande utgivet av Svenskamerikanska pressutredningen* [The Emigrants' Newspapers. Report of the Swedish Commission on the Swedish-American Press]. Mimeographed. Stockholm: Utrikesdepartementet, 1971. (Swedish Department of State stencil 1971: 1.)

Olson, Adolph A. *A Centenary History: As related to the Baptist General Conference of America*. Chicago: Baptist Conference Press, 1952.

Olsson, Karl A. *By One Spirit. A History of the Evangelical Covenant Church of America*. Chicago: Covenant Press, 1962.

Olsson, Oscar N. *The Augustana Lutheran Church in America, 1869–1910: The Formative Period*. Multilithed. Davenport, Iowa: Executive Council of Augustana Lutheran Church, 1956.

Olsson, Nils William. *Swedish Passenger Arrivals in New York, 1820–1850*. Chicago: Swedish Pioneer Historical Society, 1967.

Rice, John G. "Marriage Behavior and the Persistence of Swedish Communities in Rural Minnesota." In *Perspectives on Swedish Immigration*, pp. 136–50. Edited by Nils Hasselmo. Chicago and Duluth: Swedish Pioneer Historical Society and University of Minnesota, Duluth, 1978.

Rondahl, Björn. "Ljusne 1906—en politiskt motiverad utvandring" [Ljusne, Hälsingland, 1906: An Example of Emigration with a Political Background]. In *Utvandring. Den svenska emigrationen till Amerika i historiskt perspectiv* [Emigration. Swedish Emigration to America in Historical Perspective], pp. 119–29. Anthology edited by Ann-Sofie Kälvemark. Stockholm: Wahlström & Widstrand, 1973.

Scott, Franklin D. "The Study of the Effects of Emigration." *Scandinavian Economic History Review*, 8 (1960): 161–74.

————. "Sweden's Constructive Opposition to Emigration." *Journal of Modern History*, 37 (1965), 307–35.

Skarstedt, Ernst. *Våra Pennfäktare. Lefnads- och karaktärsteckningar öfver svenskamerikanska tidningsmän, skalder och författare* [Our Ink-Slingers. Biographical and Character Sketches of Swedish-American Journalists,

Poets and Authors]. San Francisco: Ernst Skarstedt, 1897.

Söderstrom, Alfred, ed. *Blixter på Tidnings-horisonten, samlade och Magasinerade af Alfred Soderström* [Lightning Flashes on the Newspaper Horizon. Collected and Preserved by Alfred Söderstrom]. Warroad, MN, 1910.

Stephenson, George M., trans. and ed. "Documents Relating to Peter Cassel and the Settlement at New Sweden." *Swedish-American Historical Society Bulletin*, 2, No. 1 (1929), 55–62.

——————. *The Religious Aspects of Swedish Immigration*. Minneapolis: University of Minnesota Press, 1932.

Stockenström, Göran. "Sociological Aspects of Swedish-American Literature." In *Perspectives on Swedish Immigration*, pp. 256–78. Edited by Nils Hasselmo. Chicago and Duluth: Swedish Pioneer Historical Society and University of Minnesota, Duluth, 1978.

Swanson, Alan. *"Där ute:* Moberg's Predecessors." In *Perspectives on Swedish Immigration*, pp. 279–90. Edited by Nils Hasselmo. Chicago and Duluth: Swedish Pioneer Historical Society and University of Minnesota, Duluth, 1978.

Tedebrand, Lars-Göran. "Remigration from America to Sweden." In *From Sweden to America*, pp. 201–27. Edited by Harald Runblom and Hans Norman. Minneapolis and Uppsala: University of Minnesota Press and University of Uppsala, 1976.

Thomas, Brinley. *Migration and Economic Growth*. Cambridge: Cambridge University Press. 1954.

——————. *Migration and Urban Development*. London: Methuen, 1972.

Thomas, Dorothy Swaine. *Social and Economic Aspects of Swedish Population Movements, 1750–1933*. New York: Macmillan Company, 1941.

Unonius, Gustaf. *A Pioneer in Northwest America, 1841–1858*. 2 vols. Minneapolis: University of Minnesota Press and Swedish Pioneer Historical Society, 1950, 1960.

Vedder, R. K., and Gallaway, L. E. "The Settlement Preferences of Scandinavian Emigrants to the United States, 1860–1960." *Scandinavian Economic History Review*, 18, Nos. 1–2 (1970), 159–76.

Westerberg, Wesley M. "Bethel Ship to Bishop Hill." *SPHQ*, 23, No. 2 (April 1972), 55–59.

——————. "Swedish Methodists in Chicago in the 1850s." *SPHQ*, 12, No. 4 (October 1961), 146–56.

——————. "Swedish-American Religious and Secular Organizations." In *Perspectives on Swedish Immigration*, pp. 199–205. Edited by Nils Hasselmo. Chicago and Duluth: Swedish Pioneer Historical Society and University of Minnesota, Duluth, 1978.

Westin, Gunnar. "Emigration and Scandinavian Church Life." *SPHQ*, 8, No. 2 (April 1957), 35–48.

Wittke, Carl F. "Immigration Policy Prior to World War I." In *Immigration: An American Dilemma. Problems in American Civilization*, pp. 1–10. Boston: D. C. Heath and Company, 1953.

Index

The Swedish letters *å*, *ä*, and *ö* are alphabetized as though they were *a* and *o* respectively.

without benefit of clergy and frequently in conflict with them. There he soon formed a sect of his own called the Erik Janssonists, who believed that it was possible for the believer immediately to live a sinless life. In opposition to the Lutheran position on such matters, the Janssonists went so far as to hold book burnings of devotional literature, such as the writings of Luther and Arndt, setting themselves at odds with the administration of law and order. The Janssonists became the target of repeated court hearings and official persecutions, and Jansson himself was arrested on numerous occasions and spent most of his time between 1844 and early 1846 in prison. During this time the sect began to give serious consideration to the idea of emigration, and it received some encouragement from the letters of earlier emigrants.

Among Jansson's most devoted followers were two brothers from Söderala, Olof and Jonas Olsson. Once the Janssonists had reached a decision to emigrate, Olof Olsson left for America in the fall of 1845 to make preparations for their arrival and, above all, to choose a suitable site for a settlement. In New York, Olsson consulted with the Methodist preacher Olof Gustaf Hedström, whose unrigged "Bethel Ship" lay anchored in lower Manhattan harbor. From the ship, Hedström spread Methodist teachings among newly-arrived emigrants and also provided them with practical information about travel routes and likely settlement locations. After his talk with Hedström, Olsson decided to make his way to Illinois, where Hedström's brother, Jonas, a blacksmith and wagon maker, also functioned as a lay preacher. Once in Illinois, Olsson, with Jonas Hedström's help, chose a site in Henry County, approximately 140 miles southwest of Chicago.

Meanwhile Erik Jansson had been arrested in Hälsingland for the sixth time and sent by special transport to the city prison in Gävle. En route he managed to escape to Norway, and later, by way of Copenhagen, Hamburg, and Liverpool, he sailed to New York with his family. He arrived in Illinois in the summer of 1846, when he, Olof Olsson, and a small group of earlier arrivals purchased the land in Henry County.

During the last series of persecutions, capped by Jansson's

trial and prison sentence, the Janssonists began to regard themselves as the new children of Israel. Emigration to America
became the counterpart to the Jewish exodus into the land of
Canaan. Erik Jansson's safe arrival in Illinois was all that was
needed to put these plans into motion. Janssonists in Hälsingland and neighboring provinces sold their farms and placed
their money in a collective fund, which enabled even the poorest
of the sect to make the journey. Before the end of the year
approximately four hundred persons had arrived in the New
Jerusalem in Henry County, Illinois, which took the name of
Bishop Hill after the "prophet's" own birthplace in Uppland. In
the spring of 1847, another four hundred persons arrived. In
all, between twelve hundred and fifteen hundred Janssonists left
Sweden, although the population of Bishop Hill never reached
more than eight hundred.

The newly established colony sent positive and encouraging
words to followers in Sweden. In February, 1847, for example,
one letter read: "I can now inform you that the word has been
made perfect in our midst and that all of our adversaries'
prophecies have come to naught. For the land which we have
taken is vast and wide. It is a land of plenty for earthly souls,
brimming over with milk and honey, as prophesied in Jeremiah
3:19."[3] Over the next several years, the Janssonists made their
way to America from such harbors as Gävle, Söderhamn, Stockholm, Gothenburg, and Christiana (Oslo). Not all of them
arrived safely. One ship sank shortly after departure, another
shipwrecked off the coast of Labrador, and one shipload was
decimated by cholera on the Great Lakes.

The first winter in Illinois was extremely difficult, with
people living together in dug-outs built into the sides of a ravine;
but at its end the settlers set about their new tasks with incredible
energy and self-assurance. They broke the land, built houses,
and started numerous profitable industries, including textiles,
blacksmithing, wagonmaking, furniture, lumber, and milling.
In 1858 the colony owned about fourteen thousand acres.
Bishop Hill was a collective society where all inhabitants owned a
share of the property. This was due partially to the sect's ideal of
life and partially to necessity. Their houses followed the same

collective principles and were built in masterly fashion from hand-molded brick. A good example is provided by the so-called Brick House completed in 1851, with kitchens and dining rooms on the ground floor and, on the three upper levels, seventy large rooms for single-family dwellings. Another structure which, in physical appearance, has often stood as a symbol of Bishop Hill, is the Steeple Building from 1854. These buildings have generally withstood the test of time and have in recent years undergone extensive restoration. Today the contrast between these imposing structures and those of the small surrounding community still reminds visitors of their collective origins.

These positive details, however, do not tell half of the story. By the end of the 1850s the sect was already in a state of dissolution. Disease, early withdrawals due to Erik Jansson's dictatorial leadership, and factionalism after his death had taken their toll. In May 1850 Jansson was murdered over a dispute about a marriage arrangement between his cousin and an outsider. After that the colony was managed in a more democratic fashion, primarily as a collective. Communal ownership of all property was still in force, but the new leadership soon began to speculate in capitalistic enterprises such as railroads, housing projects, coal mines, real estate ventures, wild cat banking. As a result, the general economic crisis of 1857 dealt a severe blow to the colony and forced its leadership to draw substantial loans on the original mortgages. The rest of the colony lost faith in its leadership, and in 1860 the final struggle for control began. The collective ownership principle was abandoned, and the colony's property was divided among the remaining settlers. A court case was entered against the trustees, but after a decade in the courts it was never resolved.

The Minnesota Pioneer from Önnestad

The last group of immigrants typify the staggered westward movement of Swedish Americans, which ran parallel to emigration directly from Sweden to the Middle West. In May 1851 the nineteen-year-old Hans Mattson, from Önnestad outside Kristianstad in Skåne, sailed to America with a friend of the same age. Their reasons were partly a zest for adventure and partly the knowledge that wealth and social standing had too much influence if a career would be successful in Sweden. For several years after his arrival Mattson tried his hand at different jobs and went through the process of finding himself. In 1853 he made his home in Moline, Illinois, where he was joined by the rest of the family. A fluent knowledge of English and a natural gift for leadership encouraged him in August 1853 to head a small group of Swedes anxious to find land farther west in Minnesota.

Mattson and his party first traveled by river steamer to St. Paul, where they made inquiries about settlement possibilities. From there Mattson and two of his companions made their way down the Mississippi again to the small trading post at Red Wing, populated at the time by a handful of white settlers and a tribe of Sioux Indians. They found what they were looking for along a tributary of the Mississippi two miles west of Red Wing and staked their claim to an area. After consultations with the rest of the party, it was decided that Mattson, Gustav Kempe from Västergötland, and Carl Roos from Värmland would spend the winter on the new claim. The winter was cold but short, and by early April the group had already begun spring planting.

Throughout the spring and summer the number of log cabins increased. After another year, in September 1855, came Erik Norelius, who had served as a Lutheran minister among Swedes in northwestern Indiana. By this time the colony had a population of some hundred Swedes; this was enough to form a congregation, which received the name "Vasa." The name was attractive enough, and the colony soon adopted it as its own; up to that time it had simply been called "Mattson's Settlement." Mattson began to promote the colony by writing letters to the Swedish-American newspaper, *Hemlandet,* which had subscribers on both sides of the Atlantic. This publicity, coupled with private correspondence from the Vasa colonists, led to a steady stream of immigrants over the next several years. The new arrivals were a mixed group: some immigrated directly from Sweden, while others filtered in from the East Coast as Swedish-American pioneers. Mattson himself, as he writes in his *Reminiscences,* found the "world becoming too narrow on the